Discussions of
Shakespeare's Romantic Comedy

DISCUSSIONS OF LITERATURE

Discussions of

SHAKESPEARE'S

ROMANTIC COMEDY

Edited with an Introduction by
HERBERT WEIL, JR.
University of Connecticut

D. C. HEATH AND COMPANY
BOSTON

Printed March 1966

Printed in the United States of America

Boston   Englewood   Chicago   San Francisco
Atlanta   Dallas

CONTENTS

INTRODUCTION

Many of us today find Shakespeare's comedies a delight to watch in a good production, somewhat more difficult to read, and much more difficult to talk about intelligently. For many years, plays in which a serious tone dominates and comedies with an obvious satiric or didactic purpose received the most careful and perceptive criticism. Only in the past two decades has a penetrating critical dialogue flourished about the spirit, the form, and the unity of romantic comedies with their strained love stories, far-fetched adventures, many disguises, and triumphantly happy endings.

In order to overcome the initial difficulty in discussing such generally accepted masterpieces as *Much Ado About Nothing, As You Like It,* and *Twelfth Night,* the critic may well choose one of two approaches. First, he can attempt to recapture for the reader in his study the vitality and movement of a production. When he does this, he resembles the director who concerns himself first with the immediate response of the audience before worrying about thorough, over-all interpretations. He will ask some of the questions the director poses for himself and his actors. When should the presentation change its pace or its tone? How can it use the laughter of the audience to contribute to the action? How can the straightforward line be distinguished from the ironic. The literal interpretation from the intended exaggeration? What identifies the basic atmosphere or mood of each comedy — its "world"? Although such fundamental problems can perhaps never receive precise or final solutions, we must and do come to terms with them when we watch a play. Critics who discuss them can often enlighten us about some vital aspect of a play, such as its staging, its characters, or its laughter.

Critics who adopt the second approach go beyond any response possible to us *while* we watch or read a play — and therefore, beyond our experience in the theater. They will attempt — after much "living with the play," thinking about it, wrestling with it — to find its essence: the coherence and unity to which all its other qualities are subordinated.

Critical essays which set out to formulate hypotheses about unity are very ambitious. Their authors try to explain much more than did the earlier critics who emphasized only a single element of a play: its story, clown, hero, source, or moral. For such a co-ordinating hypothesis to be completely successful, we must find it adequate for all those elements of the play that it does not discuss as well as for those that it does. Whether the critic discovers a play's unity by attention to a theme or mood, to the fable or the deeds of the hero, or to a formal pattern that guides our expectations, his conclusions must be tested by our own experience of the play. Even though a good penetrating essay may not completely convince us of its thesis, it forces us to return to the play, to understand it better, to feel it more sensitively — at the very least, to give reasons in support of our disagreement.

Because many of the best recent essays do try to achieve comprehensive interpretations, this anthology is largely devoted to examples of them. Yet the student may prefer to begin with discussions that isolate more readily accessible elements in a play. Charles Lamb and William Hazlitt share the romantic interest that emphasizes a single character rather than any unifying theme or pattern. John Palmer and Harold Goddard, two more recent critics who also stress individual characters, differ sharply in judging the moral implications of a clown's actions and statements. The brief observations by Samuel Johnson reveal how his conceptions of plot, of imitation, and of poetic justice shape and limit his responses to these plays. Still more extreme are the opinions of George Bernard Shaw, who refuses to accept Shakespeare's basic conventions and premises. In his lively attack upon what he considers to be mere appeals to a lazy public by a mercenary playwright, Shaw provides a rare example of a barely explored subject. The critical literature is entirely lacking in extended, careful arguments that might show how the romantic comedies fail. We need not agree with Shaw's judgment of these plays to profit from his irritation at "bardolatry": undiscriminating praise of all that Shakespeare ever wrote. Such blind praise can lead to forced laughter at the wrong times, to reviews that dare not criticize anything more significant than the heroine's legs, and — worst of all — to the sort of hypocrisy that can always pretend to admire even the dull line and the careless passage.

More inclusive are the methods by which David Cecil, Francis Fergusson, and C. L. Barber address the comedies. Cecil attempts to recapture the unique "world" of these plays. Unlike a critical analysis that dissects the play in searching for its underlying principles, Cecil's appreciation emphasizes mood and tone. This is an important critical task, one which some appreciations rarely go beyond, but it is also a task which more precise investigations too often ignore. By effectively contrasting the elements of construction and humor in *Much Ado About Nothing* with those in the earlier farce, *The Comedy of Errors*, Fergusson raises the fertile and relatively untapped subject of the functions of laughter in Shakespeare's "happy comedies." Barber shows how the humor in *As You Like It* protects romance from becoming shallow sentimentality.

Many readers and critics have long been accustomed to think of laughter as the distinguishing trait of comedy in general. It comes as a surprise, therefore, that there are relatively few searching and perceptive explanations of the way in which humor contributes to an entire Shakespearean comedy. To explore this subject, the critic should ask such questions as: How can a humorous scene lead us to adopt negative attitudes toward the characters or ideas it ridicules when a more direct statement of the same attitude might never convince us? Why does a scene correctly guide our responses if we laugh at it, but often mislead us if we do not find it funny? How does humor affect that other trait most often associated with comedy — the happy ending?

Perhaps one barrier to the criticism of humor has been an awareness that laughter by itself cannot be considered *the* defining characteristic of comedy. Because laughter often appears in tragedy or in any genre, its presence alone does not certify the comic form. Nor can intensity, quantity, or consistency of laughter be a primary criterion for judging comedy. We do not laugh continually at a comic work of any length, and we undoubtedly laugh harder at successful farce. Another obstacle to analysis of funny scenes has been a justifiable reluctance to explain away our enjoyment by subjecting it to an intense scrutiny. But there is no reason why, after our laughter subsides, we should not go on to try to determine the causes for our laughter and, more important for the play, the function of humor in the whole comedy.

When we do consider the funny passages closely, we soon see that our responses range from spontaneous laughter at the obvious to an intellectual recognition of incongruity or inconsistency at which we do not necessarily laugh at all. For example, after enjoying the superb malapropisms of Dogberry in *Much Ado*, the student will quickly recognize that Shakespeare has shaped the form and mood of the whole play by giving such a crucial plot function to a bumbling, pompous (but likable) clown. Other passages reveal a more subtle and complex kind of humor. The student should relish the opening lines of *Much Ado* for the good-natured fun they poke at the conceited heroes of the conventional romance and their exploits in trumped-up battles. If he recognizes this humor, he should also respond to the satire on the conventional language of lovers that opens this play as well as *A Midsummer Night's Dream* and *Twelfth Night*.

More subtle still is the brilliant manner in which the comic hero, heroine, and their friends — with whom we are clearly meant to sympathize — contradict themselves and make themselves seem foolish. Here we have an intellectual humor — one that often is not accompanied by laughter. In *As You Like It*, for example, Celia chatters to Rosalind that the women Fortune "makes fair she scarce makes honest, and those she makes honest, she makes very ill-favoredly," (I.ii.36.). Since we must assume that the romantic heroine is fair, Celia seems to be saying that she cannot be chaste. But of course she does not mean what her statement implies. Our recognition of this incongruity suggests to us how, in comedy, the literal statement and the logical implication give us only part of the truth.

Similarly, in the melodramatic opening scene of *As You Like It*, the hero, Orlando — who is persecuted, but clearly good — attempts to defend his father's honor against his brother and tormentor, the dastardly Oliver: "He is thrice a villain that says such a father begets villains," (I.i.53.). That we note Orlando's explicit but unconscious condemnation of himself (when he calls his brother a villain), does not for a moment confuse us or lessen our sympathy with the verbally befuddled good son. But this slight touch does make the characterization more suggestive — and may offer us a perspective upon the flatness of the conventional hero in similar plays. If the reader thinks these points could easily be missed, he should realize that a director and actor can readily call our attention to such nuances. The main action of the play makes sense without their recognition, but they add an extra dimension of complexity and delight.

Just as our laughter should lead us to understand more than the literal content of the passages, our response to structure should extend beyond a mere recognition of how the play concludes. Few spectators of these three plays need help to see that the story will end happily, that the hero will wed the heroine, that all apparent dangers and threats of evil obstacles will be overcome. The threats to Orlando's life by Oliver and the wrestler, the alleged drowning of Sebastian, the military exploits that have supposedly endangered Claudio and Benedick, all come early in the action and barely disturb or impress us. In *Much Ado About Nothing*, *As You Like It*, and *Twelfth Night*, we relax into comic curiosity rather than feel melodramatic suspense over *what* will happen. In attempting to understand the structure of comedy we may try to explain how the "optimistic" expectations of reader or spectator are shaped from moment to moment. That, in *Much Ado*, Dogberry first appears just before the cruel accusation and pretended death of Hero clearly influences our mood and our expectations. Perhaps this is because he brings with him a sort of wild hilarity that discourages any moral judgment of his character and that is quite unlike any humor earlier in the play. Our laughter at Dogberry's foolish mistakes — including his defense of the villain Don John — does not prove to us that Hero's swoon is remediable. But it does limit our concern, and it adds a sense of rightness when first Hero and finally Claudio's love revive. Our laughter helps create the mood suited to the happy ending. As Eric Bentley has argued, such an ending is

> not ironical, it is in effect, spread throughout the play; . . . it is a fitting culmination.
>
> . . . . .
>
> The happy ending of a romantic comedy is somehow implicit from the beginning . . . it is an effect of enchantment in the shape of an apparent realization of our fondest hopes — that is, our hopes for love and happiness.

The surprise appropriate to these comedies grows not from an exciting fable but from variations on familiar and conventional plots. When the apparent hero — noble, generous, and lovelorn — in the opening scene of *Twelfth Night* adores the mourning, scornful Olivia, we naturally expect them to wed. And so they do. But not each other. That Orsino and Olivia marry the twin brother and sister they had never met (or even heard of) as the play opened, embroils us in a series of disguises, (as Professor Summers stresses) and places severe demands upon the power of many modern readers to suspend their disbelief. The reader must accept such conventions as love-at-first-sight, abnormal stresses placed on that love, sudden conversions of villains, and the possibility of mistaking a girl for a boy — a mistake that of course becomes a more complex and intricate joke because the Elizabethan theater used boys to play the parts of all young girls.

Once we become familiar with these traditional devices and put aside our demands for a realistic story, we are better prepared to understand the "romance" game being played in these comedies. Remembering that these conventions always remained rather loose and were not accepted as inflexible rules, we will be able to recognize the finesse with which Shakespeare used them while also altering — and often parodying — them. Olivia's role in *Twelfth Night* posed problems which could easily have led a lesser dramatist to make her not only fickle and foolish, but also colorless and two-dimensional. She must be a virtuous woman who will: 1) replace her mourning with an impossible love — for Viola in disguise; 2) marry Sebastian, whom she has just met; and 3) retain our sympathy and attention without overshadowing the other heroine, Viola. Some readers may find that the resulting character has been sifted through so many conventions and limitations by Shakespeare that it is in danger of becoming anonymous. But if we resist an unduly earnest literalism, we can see how well he has solved the problems to which Olivia's role leads. He has mildly ridiculed her for her excessive mourning over her dead brother — a ridicule she accepts with good humor. His romance plot allows her to switch her love from Viola to Sebastian with as little change in the essential object of her love as is logically possible. We might say that he has suggested that Olivia loves the essence beneath the appearance of Viola, an essense which, in this rare world of Illyria, can be reproduced in the free and available Sebastian.

Comedy and romance blend here: we can laugh without excessive cruelty; we can retain our sympathies without misleading doubts; and we can confidently await the resolution with the reappearance of Sebastian. As in *Much Ado* and *As You Like It,* Shakespeare has added to the humor and confidence typical of comedy, a fertile inclusiveness — surprising variations in plot, character, and theme — and a complex perspective that allows him to use a device or convention quite seriously at some moments and at other times to poke fun at the same convention. The ridicule of simple-minded romance in the jesting of Benedick and Beatrice, in the sallies of Touchstone and Jaques, of Sir Toby and Feste — of almost every clown, hero, and heroine in Shakespeare's comedy — provide examples of this complex, inclusive view. Such a view — like the humorous scenes and like Helen Gardner's idea of the essence of comedy as "an image of life triumphing over chance" — makes the happy ending seem appropriate. Even a limited familiarity with these ideas about comedy should help the student recognize how they operate in individual plays.

In order to provide several interpretations of each comedy, the focus of this volume is limited to three plays — those romantic comedies usually considered most successful by both audiences and critics. Only *A Midsummer Night's Dream* and *The Merchant of Venice* have achieved popularity comparable to that of the three plays discussed here. And as David Cecil notes, the former with its increased fantasy and the latter with its more ominous threats, move away from the main-stream of romantic comedy.

The problems of story, of character, and of seriousness posed by *Much Ado About Nothing* seem accessible to the student after his first reading. The three essays reprinted here go far beyond the earlier debates over the historical or conventional justification for Claudio's cruelty toward his fiancée to answer the charges that the play lacks unity or coherence. Francis Fergusson effectively shows the increasing skill and complexity of Shakespeare's craft as he constructs his actions upon subtle and shifting relations between multiple plots. A. P. Rossiter and Graham Storey search for a unifying idea or theme rather than a controlling tone or genre. These two articles complement each other well even though both find central the theme of man's giddiness or inconstancy. Storey devotes most of his attention to Shakespeare's careful planning and to the highly emotional church scene which threatens to destroy the comic outlook. Rossiter, on the other hand, emphasizes the wit of Benedick and Beatrice and "the equivocal quality of the greatest comedy" which approaches the "point where a sense of humor fails; where to see life and the world in humorous proportions is no longer possible."

Two of the discussions of *As You Like It* generalize about the whole play; the other two, by John Palmer and Harold C. Goddard, focus upon character. Helen Gardner shows with brilliant economy that *As You Like It* relies for its success far less upon humor and story — upon intrigues and complications — than do *Much Ado* and *Twelfth Night*. She thinks the significant movement of the play lies in fantasy and coincidence rather than in logic or plot. C. L. Barber shows how the humor of the critical intelligence mocks the romantic ideals presented in the play; consequently, our laughter leads us to observe, even in the more artificial scenes, an "important realism toward the subject of romance."

In all four essays on *Twelfth Night*, the authors attempt to formulate the central metaphor, pattern, or thematic problem of the play. G. K. Hunter's discussion, beginning with an effective comparison of the fools and heroine in *Twelfth Night* with those in *As You Like It*, goes on to interpret the play as a pattern or dance in which the lovers are simply rotated until they are paired — a formula that requires from them little learning or improvement. L. G. Salingar shows, for each of the four romantic characters in the main plot, how thoroughly Shakespeare has modified the "realistic" characterization and motivation found in his sources. Unlike Hunter, Salingar feels that this quartet presents "a general, subtle composite picture of true love." Joseph Summers demonstrates that the multiple disguises lead to a continuing concern with the nature of identity and of role, culminating in a "clear-eyed and affirmative vision." John Hollander argues that the plot carefully develops the metaphor of moral indulgence and its purging through satiety. He concludes that Shakespeare rejects, by his use of a moral process, the static system of the Jonsonian humors. His argument leads clearly to the final generalizing essay by Frye, who works from a similar distinction between Jonsonian and Shakespearean comedy to suggest that Shakespeare's work is "far more primitive and popular, and is of a type found all over the world," in Mozart, in Gilbert and Sullivan, and in countless movies.

Good criticism will prove most valuable to those readers who already enjoy the comedies but who cannot explain the causes for their pleasure.

Not even sound, stimulating criticism can create enjoyment, but it can clear away obstacles that arise from misunderstandings, from viewing the plays from the wrong perspectives, from asking questions inappropriate to the form of the work and the intentions of the writer. In particular, good criticism can help us avoid two very basic errors in our interpretation of comedy — the assumptions that the comic mode should be either completely frivolous or else that it should be unduly serious.

It is surprising that in our "enlightened" age of uncensored expression there is still a strong puritanical current which insists that matters presented in a non-serious mode should therefore not have serious implications or meanings. For much too long the criticism of comedy has been crippled by the assumption that all the characters and language in comedy must be low, and that therefore no serious ideas can be introduced. Such a view can too easily lead to rejection of the comic work by the moralist.

The other extreme attitude ignores both form and context to treat the ideas, the characters, and the language of comedy with inappropriate seriousness. For example, in his *Shakespeare Our Contemporary,* the book on Shakespeare's work most widely discussed in 1964, Jan Kott argues that *A Midsummer Night's Dream* is no pleasant romance but primarily a drama of "cruel and scatological humor" — often about "animal eroticism." Surely most of us would agree that this interpretation distorts the spirit of Shakespeare's play, but to eliminate completely such distortions in our own readings poses a difficult challenge.

Many contemporary readers and writers pride themselves on their freedom from "romantic sentimentality." The hard surface of many characters in Hemingway stories and Bogart movies — not to mention their popular but inferior imitations — implies that they know the score, that they possess a strong-willed control which excludes the weak and cloying. But often this convention only misleads. Under the tough outer shell there frequently lies a thoroughly sentimental core. In a far richer and more complex vein, Shakespeare used the fable, characters and conventions of romance; he deepened them by explicitly pointing out their absurdities and incompleteness as a total response to life. In so doing, he created some of the best examples of actions that — without either cutting deeply or tormenting our spirits — can suggest for us both the limitations and the promises of romantic comedy.

Notes and Suggestions for Further Reading

There are few full-length books on Shakespeare's comedies. In addition to C. L. Barber's *Shakespeare's Festive Comedy* (1959), John Russell Brown's *Shakespeare and His Comedies* (1957), which emphasizes unifying themes, deserves particular attention. Bertrand Evans in *Shakespeare's Comedies* (1960) bases his discussion on the "discrepant awareness" among the characters and between characters and audience. H. B. Charlton's *Shakespearean Comedy* (1938), long the best-known book on the subject, stresses Shakespeare's use of his sources; in this connection, the student can find useful reprints of original works and translations in Geoffrey Bullough's *Narrative and Dramatic Sources of Shakespeare,* Volumes I and II (1957, 1958). J. Dover Wilson collects many of his earlier ideas in *Shakespeare's Happy Comedies* (1962). *A Natural Perspective* (1965) by Northrop Frye is a development and application of ideas that the author had discussed in widely scattered essays, including the final selection of this book.

Especially suggestive general studies are Northrop Frye's *Anatomy of Criticism* (1957), his "The Argument of Comedy" which has often been reprinted from *English Institute Essays* (1948–9), Suzanne Langer's *Feeling and Form* (1953), and Eric Bentley's *The Life of the Drama* (1964). More specialized are E. C. Pettet's *Shakespeare and the Romance Tradition* (1949), and Rufus A. Blanshard's sprightly and brief corrective to academic earnestness, "Shakespeare's Funny Comedy," in *College English* XXI (1959).

For discussions of *Much Ado About Nothing,* the student might consider, in addition to the books on Shakespearean comedy, chapters in M. C. Bradbrook's *Shakespeare and Elizabethan Poetry* (1951) and E. K. Chambers' *Shakespeare: A Survey* (1925). Emphases quite different from those in this collection may be found in Charles T. Prouty's *The Sources of "Much Ado About Nothing"* (1951), Barbara Everett's *Much Ado About Nothing* in *Critical Quarterly,* III (1961), 319–51, and Charles A. Owen Jr.'s "Comic Awareness, Style, and Dramatic Technique in *Much Ado About Nothing*," *Boston University Studies in English,* V (1961), 193–207. The student should also consult James A. S. McPeek's "The Thief Deformed," *Boston University Studies in English,* IV (1960), pp. 65–84, and Kirby Neill's "Much Ado About Claudio: An Acquittal for the Slandered Groom," *Shakespeare Quarterly,* III (1952), 91–107 as well as T. W. Craik's "Much Ado About Nothing" in *Scrutiny* xix (1953), 293–316.

Fewer issues have developed in the criticism of *As You Like It,* but particularly sensible is Harold Jenkins' *As You Like It, Shakespeare Survey* 8 (1955), 40–51. Many of his sound observations on juxtaposition of plots and characters have been used in the essay by Miss Gardner included in this collection. James Smith's *As You Like It* in *Scrutiny*, IX (1940), 9–32; Oscar J. Campbell's *Shakespeare's Satire* (1943); S. L. Bethell's discussion of Touchstone in *Shakespeare and the Popular Dramatic Tradition* (1944), 92–6; and Marco Mincoff's "What Shakespeare Did to Rosalynde," *Shakespeare Jahrbuch*, XCV (1960), 78–89, have influenced later studies of the play.

For *Twelfth Night*, the student should consider the opinions of A. C. Bradley, "Feste the Jester" in *A Book of Homage to Shakespeare* (1916), 164–9; Enid Welsford's *The Fool: His Social and Literary History* (1935), and Alan Downer's "Feste's Night," *College English*, XIII (1952), 258–68. Sylvan Barnet in his study, "Charles Lamb and the Tragic Malvolio," *Philological Quarterly* XXXIII (1954), 177–88, and Leslie Hotson, *The First Night of Twelfth Night* (1954) demonstrate quite different but fascinating types of historical detective-work; Norman Holland in *The Shakespearean Imagination* (1964) studies psychological implications of the play, while Ngaio Marsh offers a particularly helpful "Note on the Production of *Twelfth Night*," *Shakespeare Survey* 8 (1953), 69–73.

Herbert Weil, Jr.

notes on the
CONTRIBUTORS

C. L. Barber, Professor and Chairman of the Department of English at Indiana University, has written *Shakespeare's Festive Comedy* (1959) and more recent studies of Shakespeare, Marlow, and Milton.

Lord David Cecil is Goldsmith Professor of English Literature at Oxford. Among his widely varied publications are *Early Victorian Novelists* (1934), *The Younger Melbourne* (1939), and *The Fine Art of Reading* (1957).

Francis Fergusson, Professor of English at Rutgers University, is author of the influential *The Idea of a Theater* (1950), *Dante's Drama of the Mind* (1953), and *The Human Image in Dramatic Literature* (1957).

Northrop Frye, Principal of Victoria College, the University of Toronto, includes among his influential works *Fearful Symmetry: A Study of William Blake* (1947), *Anatomy of Criticism* (1957), and, most recently, *A Natural Perspective* (1965).

Helen Gardner is Reader in Renaissance Literature at Oxford and the author of *The Art of T. S. Eliot* (1949), and *The Business of Criticism* (1960). She has edited the poems of John Donne.

Harold C. Goddard (1878–1950), former President of Swarthmore College and Professor of English, wrote the posthumously published *The Meaning of Shakespeare* (1951).

William Hazlitt (1778–1830) was one of the most important 19th century critics of Shakespeare. Among his best known writings are *The Characters of Shakespeare's Plays* (1817), *Lectures on the English Poets* (1818), and *Lectures on the Comic Writers of Great Britain* (1819).

John Hollander teaches at Yale. Among his published poetry and criticism are *A Crackling of Thorns* (1958), *The Untuning of the Sky* (1961), and *Movie-Going* (1962).

G. K. Hunter, Professor of English at the University of Warwick, has written *John Lyly: The Humanist as Courtier* (1962) and *Shakespeare: The Later Comedies* (1962); he edited the excellent New Arden edition of *All's Well That Ends Well*.

Samuel Johnson (1709–84), in addition to his many other critical works, wrote the most-often quoted essay of his century on Shakespeare, the Preface to his edition of Shakespeare (1765). His valuable Notes and General Observations comprise part of this edition.

Charles Lamb (1775–1834), best remembered as a familiar essayist, wrote several influential short pieces on Shakespeare which were included in the *Essays of Elia* (1822).

John Palmer (1885–1944), a diplomat as well as a critic, was author of *The Comedy of Manners* (1913), *Ben Jonson* (1934), and *Political and Comic Characters of Shakespeare* (1945–6).

A. P. Rossiter, before his death in 1957, delivered at Stratford the lectures collected in *Angel With Horns* (1961) — one of the most stimulating recent books on Shakespeare. He taught at Cambridge and wrote *English Drama from Early Times to the Elizabethans* (1950).

L. G. Salingar, contributor of many articles to the Pelican *Guide to English Literature*, is currently working on a book about Shakespeare's comedy. He teaches at Cambridge.

George Bernard Shaw (1856–1950), in addition to his own plays and prefaces, wrote innumerable reviews of music and the theatre. Many of the latter are collected in *Our Theatres in the Nineties* (1931) and in *Shaw on Shakespeare*, edited by Edwin Wilson (1961).

Graham Storey, editor of *Angel With Horns* (1961), teaches at Cambridge.
Joseph H. Summers, Professor of English at Washington University, is the author of *George Herbert: His Religion and Art* (1954), and *The Muse's Method: An Introduction to Paradise Lost* (1962). He has also edited *Marvell: Selected Poems* (1961).

Herbert Weil, Jr. teaches at the University of Connecticut and has recently completed a study of Shakespeare's comic method in *Measure for Measure*.

DAVID CECIL

Shakespearean Comedy

"SHAKESPEAREAN COMEDY" is not the same thing as "Shakespeare's Comedies." "Shakespeare's Comedies" has come to mean all those of his plays that end happily. These are a very mixed lot, ranging from boisterous farces like *The Taming of the Shrew* to grave romances like *The Tempest* and powerful problem dramas like *Measure for Measure*. "Shakespearean Comedy," on the other hand, means the great comedies of Shakespeare's early maturity — *A Midsummer-Night's Dream, The Merchant of Venice, Much Ado About Nothing, As You Like It, Twelfth Night,* with their precursors *Love's Labour's Lost* and *The Two Gentlemen of Verona;* and these plays, though unlike each other in many ways, have certain basic characteristics in common which make them a definable, recognizable genre.

A genre, moreover, in which Shakespeare alone is a master. For the other great comedy of the world's literature, the comedy of Molière or Ben Jonson, is different in kind to his. It is satirical and intellectual, its aim is to mock some particular vice or folly; and it is rationally constructed so that every character and episode has its necessary part to play in fulfilling this aim. Not so Shakespeare's. The form of his comedies is loose and the different elements in it are not integrated by any intellectual principle at all. Here they are like other Elizabethan plays. These were primarily entertainments; and any element could be admitted to them which seemed likely to make them entertaining. The line between comedy and tragedy even, was vague. All we can say is that in the tragedies the dramatist seeks to entertain mainly by playing on our capacity to shudder and shed tears; whereas in the comedies the Elizabethan dramatist sets out to entertain by playing on our lighter, gayer feelings, whether humorous or sentimental. Shakespeare's come-

From *The Fine Art of Reading* by Lord David Cecil, copyright © 1957, by Richard Michael Ritchie and the Most Honourable Robert Arthur James Marquess of Salisbury K.G., P.C., reprinted by permission of the publishers, The Bobbs-Merrill Company, Inc., and Constable & Co., Ltd. This selection is Part I of the essay "Shakespearean Comedy."

dies are a hotch-potch of all the different elements which constituted "light" entertainment for an Elizabethan audience.

First of all, holding the fabric together, there is the plot. It is never a probable, true-to-life plot, nor is it meant to be. Shakespeare's aim is to take us out of real life into a more agreeable imaginative region. The setting may be called Venice or Athens. But there is no attempt to make it a realistic picture of these places: each stands for some exotic fairy-tale country, some Never-Never Land that appeals to the imagination just because it is unlike the ordinary humdrum England in which his audience was living. The same is true of its inhabitants, at least of those characters round which the plot revolves. Hero and heroine alike are figures of romance, beautiful, gallant and witty, and with the charm of their personalities enhanced by the associations of high station. They are kings and queens, princes and princesses, dukes and duchesses. Doctor Johnson said, "A man would be as happy in the arms of a chambermaid as of a duchess were it not for imagination." Shakespeare clearly agreed with him: when creating a heroine whose charms are to appeal to our imagination, he makes her something like a duchess.

Again, the plots in which these characters take part are fanciful to the last degree. Since Shakespeare is catering for an audience who has come to the theatre to be taken out of their own lives and not to see the sort of events that happen in their own lives, he chooses stories that turn on some fantastic hypothesis: a brother and sister so alike that, if dressed the same, they can be taken for each other: a man wagering a pound of his own flesh to oblige a friend: a girl deceiving her own father and lover in the disguise of a boy. And the emotion that actuates the chief characters is also romantic. It is love; again, not a realistic picture of the passion in all its troubled variety, but love in its lighter more agreeable aspects, its prettiness and its absurdity — love as depicted by the court poet, and decorated with all manner of courtly graces. Blind Cupid shoots an arrow, his victim immediately forgets every other consideration: obsessed and exhilarated by his passion, like someone under a magic spell, he sets forth in pursuit of the beloved object. And if Cupid shoots at him afresh, he will change his object in the twinkling of an eye and without a moment's compunction.

This plot determines the general framework of the play, but into it are fitted any other elements which Shakespeare and the contemporaries thought likely to enrich and diversify their sense of pleasure. There is an Elizabethan phrase I read somewhere, "A Paradise of Dainty Delights." The phrase well describes the comedies, except that daintiness is not an essential. Any delight has a right to be admitted to the paradise. Broad farce, for instance: this is confined to a group of characters and generally of a lower social station. They are also drawn in a more realistic convention than the hero and heroine, caricatured pictures of English people of the period. Their very names are often English: Dogberry, Sir Toby Belch, Bottom the weaver and Audrey the milkmaid. Unlike the principals, they speak in prose and make a number of topical allusions and jokes of a robust coarseness. Such action as they are involved in is knock-about and farcical. They provide an earthy contrast to the ethereal lyrical atmosphere which trembles round the principals.

Wit provides another strain in Shakepeare's comic symphony; the quips and repartee and puns and word play, popular among the clever and elegant of Shakespeare's age. Above all there is the poetry. Poetry is of the very texture of these plays. By its incantation is the mood induced that may make us accept the extravagance and fantasy of the plot. And it is poetry carefully designed for this purpose; light, sweet, lyrical, playful, it never strikes the deeper notes in the poetic orchestra. There is no brass in it: all is flute and violin. Finally, and in addition to the music of the verse, there is the actual music. The singers and instrumental players were essential members of a Shakespearean company. In these plays, Shakespeare gives them more opportunity than anywhere else except his last romances. Moreover, the music is made an integral part of the play. The songs, as it were, crystallize the sentiment which is diffused over the whole drama. In *As You Like It* they are wood notes wild that tell of the pleasure of the countryside and proclaim its superiority to the disillusioning complications of urban life. In *Twelfth Night* they sing of the fleetingness and tenderness and frail sweetness of love. So also does the single song in *Much Ado About Nothing*. And the fact that love is the motive force in these plays, makes their musical element particularly appropriate. For all the characters, as much as for Orsino in *Twelfth Night,* "music be the food of love." Indeed, it is easier to find an analogy to Shakespeare's comedies in musical compositions than in classical comedy proper. Shakespeare the comedian is closer to Mozart than to Molière. And his descendants to-day are not the authors of drawing-room comedy but of operetta; the sort of operetta that is set in a Ruritanian court where the hero and heroine are a prince and princess divided for two acts by some misunderstanding but united happily in the third, and whose sentimental raptures are voiced in strains of voluptuous waltz music and relieved by scenes where red-nosed comedians entertain the audience by knock-about farce and broad jokes and topical allusions. In type, if not in artistic quality, *Twelfth Night* has more in common with *The Merry Widow* than with *You Never Can Tell*.

Not that we can use the word "type" of Shakespeare's comedies except in a loose sense. For though they all contain the same elements, these are mixed in very varying proportions. At one end of the scale is *A Midsummer-Night's Dream*. Here all the elements are present in their most extreme form: the farce is more farcical, the fantasy more fantastic, the relation to ordinary life even slighter and more tenuous than in the others. At the furthest remove from *A Midsummer-Night's Dream* stands *The Merchant of Venice.* Here the plot is such as to make the play only just scrape into the comedy category. The story is romantic and improbable enough but, involving as it does, the danger of a horrible death to one of the characters, it touches effectively on emotions out of harmony with the comedy atmosphere. *Much Ado About Nothing* runs a similar risk; the sub-plot is potentially a painful one. *Twelfth Night* and *As You Like It* represent the central norm of the type. All the elements appear in them, but not so etherealized as in *A Midsummer-Night's Dream* nor blended with melodrama as in *The Merchant of Venice* and *Much Ado About Nothing.*

It is to be wondered how so heterogeneous and incongruous a mixture of elements as is in these plays could ever combine into a satisfactory work of art. As a matter of fact, in the hands of most Elizabethan dramatists they did not. Their comedies, though sprinkled with humour and poetry, are too scrappy to be admired as wholes. But Shakespeare takes these flimsy bundles of scraps and, by the action of his genius, transfigures them into major works of art. Unity he achieves by suffusing his whole scene by a strong and individual quality of imagination whose distinctive characteristic it is to blend continuously humour and poetry. This makes the characters, though drawn in different conventions, inhabitants of the same world. Touchstone the clown is poetical, Rosalind the heroine humorous; absurd Sir Andrew Aguecheek touches us, pathetic Viola makes us smile. The texture of each scene is like shot silk, dark under one light, bright under another, as it shifts and shimmers in the movement of the drama. In Lodge's *Rosalynde,* from which Shakespeare takes the plot of *As You Like It,* the heroine is always serious. By flooding her and the world in which she lives with the quivering, gleaming, sparkling light of his laughter and poetry, Shakespeare both harmonizes the whole into one and makes us accept more easily the fantastic improbability of the story.

All the same — and this is the second aspect of his achievement — he gives it substance and life; the substance and life of the characters. We believe in a story because we believe in the people in it. They are individuals whose voices and manner we recognize: Shakespeare brings them to life by a thousand little strokes of observation. But, except in isolated cases such as Shylock, he takes care never to do so in such a way as to be out of keeping with his chosen comedy mood. The elements of real human nature, which he uses in order to vitalize them are all elements that are not discordant with the general lyrical key in which the whole is composed. They are made up of the comic and pretty features of human character; the graver and the more prosaic aspects are alike excluded. "Rosalind," says Bernard Shaw, "is not a complete human being. She is simply an extension in five acts of the most affectionate, fortunate, beautiful five minutes in the life of a charming woman." The same is true of Beatrice and Portia and Viola and the rest.

As with the characters, so with their feelings. The gaiety and folly and pensive sentiment of love are portrayed to the life; but not its pain, its mystery, its profounder influence on the character of the lover. If there is a moment of anxiety or sorrow, it passes, and leaves no mark when things go well again. Melancholy Antonio is not very melancholy at the end of *The Merchant of Venice* though he has been in danger of a dreadful death twenty-four hours before. It is enough for Claudio to murmur a few words of apology to Hero for her instantly to forgive him for having publicly insulted her in the most brutal fashion. Nor do we feel either character unconvincing. For in neither case has emotion been so powerfully conveyed as to make its swift disappearance incredible. The characters are real but only as real as is consistent with the exigencies of the plot. The key is always light.

Within it, however, there is great variety of tone. Viola and Toby, Rosalind and Touchstone and Jaques, Titania, Helena and Bottom — how many moods these represent! more moods, indeed, than can be found in satirical comedy. Shakespeare is in this sense truer to life than Molière or Ben Jonson. Wit and poetry, laughter and sentiment, farce and fantasy, even a touch of pensive pathos, chase one another across the surface of these plays as naturally as sunshine and shadow over a stream on a breezy day of spring.

And the stream is not a shallow stream. It is here that Shakespeare's genius shows itself most wonderfully. He gives his plays not only unity and vitality, he gives them depth. They make a profound comment on existence. Not a moral comment like the comedies of Ben Jonson! Shakespeare, indeed, has his morality. He disapproves of spite and hardheartedness, he mocks at vanity. He approves faithfulness and generosity of heart. Good sense also: Orsino's sentimentality, Jaques' misanthropy, are shown up for the immoderate absurdities they are, in the light of the genial smile with which they are portrayed. Yet these moral judgments are, as it were, by-products of Shakespeare's work, the involuntary and incidental utterance of his natural preference, not the living centre of his inspiration. His comic vision reveals itself much less in them than in his penetrating and cheerful perception of the incorrigible weakness of the human condition. For he uses the fantastic far-fetched turns of his stories as parables to illustrate his conviction that all men, from the highest to the lowest, are the creatures of chance and circumstance. Wisely or foolishly, they plan their futures, always are these plans defeated by some casual, unpredictable turn of events. Either something happens they could not have expected, or they — generally because Cupid has shot one of his arrows at them — upset their plans themselves. "'Tis but fortune; all is fortune," says Malvolio. It was true of him, it was equally true of everybody else in Shakespeare's comic world.

Shakespeare's distinctive vein of humour springs from this realization. Man, he says, is comic because he is, of his nature, a victim of illusions. This is obviously true of his farcical figures. Pompous, conscientious Malvolio imagines his fastidious mistress is in love with him; silly cowardly Sir Andrew sets up as a dashing young gallant; fussy illiterate Dogberry expects to be treated as a formidable officer of state; Bottom the weaver thinks he has the ability to play all the parts in *Pyramus and Thisbe* from the lion to the heroine. But the romantic characters are equally the victims of illusion. Orsino thinks he is in love with Olivia when he is merely in love with love: Olivia loves Viola, thinking her to be a man: Beatrice, who professes to scorn all men, is tricked by a few words into giving her heart to Benedick. The more thoughtful characters in the plays observe this propensity to illusion in their fellows and comment on it. But they, too, are victims of the very error they perceive in others. Benedick and Jaques do not realize that they are as absurd and inconsistent as those whom they mock so wittily. The wisest of the human race are those like Rosalind and Viola who recognize their congenital weakness and accept it — who do not try to mould their fortunes but follow where fate leads them.

This strain of ironical wisdom in their creator gives substance and weight to the feather-light fabric of the poetry: and the humour that it engenders is that profoundest kind of humour that proceeds from a sense of a basic incongruity in the nature of the human condition. Shakespeare does not laugh at individual men because they are weak or vain or affected. No — he laughs at all mankind, himself included; because their very essence is a bundle of contradictions, born to desire something they will never get, or that will never satisfy them if they did get it; because they are a mixture of body and soul, each always at odds with the other.

Taken as a whole, the universe is absurd [says Walter Bagehot in the most penetrating words I have ever read about Shakespeare's humour]. There seems an unalterable contradiction between the human mind and its employments. How can a *soul* be a merchant? What relation to an immortal being have the price of linseed, the fall of butter, the tare on tallow, or the brokerage on hemp? Can an undying creature debit "petty expenses," and charge for "carriage paid"? All the world's a stage; — "the satchel, and

the shining morning face" — the "strange oaths"; — "the bubble reputation"
— the

> Eyes severe and beard of formal cut,
> Full of wise saws and modern instances.

Can these things be real? Surely they are acting. What relation have they
to the truth as we see it in theory? What connection with our certain hopes,
"In respect of itself, it is a good life; but in respect it is a shepherd's life,
it is nought." The soul ties its shoes; the mind washes its hands in a basin.
All is incongruous.

But the depth that we perceive in these plays is not only the depth of
Shakespeare's humorous vein: It is also a depth of sentiment springing
paradoxically from the very lightness of his intentions. These plays are
the expression of his sense of pleasure, ordinary straightforward normal
pleasure, not joy or enraptured exaltation. But pleasure can stir profound
reflections if a profound mind contemplates it. Shakespeare had such a
mind. For the intensity of his contemplation brings along with it an
extraordinary sense of the transience and fragility of things human. He
draws a curtain and discloses to us a fairyland of youthful carefree
gaiety, all made up of jokes and song and light love footing it with one
another in tireless dance. Then for a moment Jaques philosophizes,
Rosalind remembers her dead sister, Feste sings a song, and we are
aware that, with unerring finger, Shakespeare has struck a note that
reveals he knows it all to be a shadow play that will pass — alas, how
quickly! And this gaiety is made poignant by a sense of its fleetingness,
that sets our thoughts roving into darker regions far beyond the apparent
compass of the play. As these bright figures and airy music will vanish,
so, we perceive, will the carefree mood which they embodied. The
pleasure of life is as ephemeral as a dream. All Shakespeare's comedies
might be called "Midsummer-Night's Dreams"; and its last speech might
be the last speech in all of them:

> If we shadows have offended,
> Think but this, and all is mended,
> That you have but slumber'd here
> While these visions did appear.

Such moments of realization are not harsh or discordant; the dance
goes on, the pulsing lilting rhythm does not flag. But the melody modu-
lates into a minor key to be touched with a wistful sadness. The fair
faces grow pensive, as for an instant there passes over them the shadow
of their mortality.

SAMUEL JOHNSON

General Observations on the Comedies

AS YOU LIKE IT

OF THIS PLAY the fable is wild and pleasing. I know not how the ladies will approve the facility with which both Rosalind and Celia give away their hearts. To Celia much may be forgiven for the heroism of her friendship. The character of Jaques is natural and well preserved. The comic dialogue is very sprightly, with less mixture of low buffoonery than in some other plays; and the graver part is elegant and harmonious. By hastening to the end of his work, Shakespeare suppressed the dialogue between the usurper and the hermit, and lost an opportunity of exhibiting a moral lesson in which he might have found matter worthy of his highest powers.

TWELFTH NIGHT

THIS PLAY is in the graver part elegant and easy, and in some of the lighter scenes exquisitely humorous. Aguecheek is drawn with great propriety, but his character is, in a great measure, that of natural fatuity, and is therefore not the proper prey of a satirist. The soliloquy of Malvolio is truly comic; he is betrayed to ridicule merely by his pride. The marriage of Olivia, and the succeeding perplexity, though well enough contrived to divert on the stage, wants credibility, and fails to produce the proper instruction required in the drama, as it exhibits no just picture of life.

Reprinted from Samuel Johnson's edition of *The Plays of William Shakespeare*, London, 1765. Some spelling and punctuation have been modernized.

CHARLES LAMB

The Virtues of Malvolio

THE PART of Malvolio, in the *Twelfth Night,* was performed by Bensley
with a richness and a dignity, of which (to judge from some recent
castings of that character) the very tradition must be worn out from the
stage. No manager in those days would have dreamed of giving it to
Mr. Baddely, or Mr. Parsons; when Bensley was occasionally absent
from the theatre, John Kemble thought it no derogation to succeed to
the part. Malvolio is not essentially ludicrous. He becomes comic but
by accident. He is cold, austere, repelling; but dignified, consistent, and,
for what appears, rather of an over-stretched morality. Maria describes
him as a sort of Puritan; and he might have worn his gold chain with
honour in one of our old roundhead families, in the service of a
Lambert, or a Lady Fairfax. But his morality and his manners are
misplaced in Illyria. He is opposed to the proper *levities* of the piece,
and falls in the unequal contest. Still his pride, or his gravity (call it
which you will), is inherent, and native to the man, not mock or affected,
which latter only are the fit objects to excite laughter. His quality is at
the best unlovely, but neither buffoon nor contemptible. His bearing is
lofty, a little above his station, but probably not much above his deserts.
We see no reason why he should not have been brave, honourable,
accomplished. His careless committal of the ring to the ground (which
he was commissioned to restore to Cesario), bespeaks a generosity of
birth and feeling. His dialect on all occasions is that of a gentleman and
a man of education. We must not confound him with the eternal old,
low steward of comedy. He is master of the household to a great
princess; a dignity probably conferred upon him for other respects than
age or length of service. Olivia, at the first indication of his supposed
madness, declares that she "would not have him miscarry for half of
her dowry." Does this look as if the character was meant to appear little
or insignificant? . . .

Reprinted from "On Some of the Old Actors," originally published in *The London Magazine,*
1822; revised in *Essays of Elia,* 1823; in *The Life and Works of Charles Lamb,* ed. Alfred
Ainger, Vol. II (1899), 259–65. Title of this selection provided by present editor.

Bensley, accordingly, threw over the part an air of Spanish loftiness. He looked, spake, and moved like an old Castilian. He was starch, spruce, opinionated, but his superstructure of pride seemed bottomed upon a sense of worth. There was something in it beyond the coxcomb. It was big and swelling, but you could not be sure that it was hollow. You might wish to see it taken down, but you felt that it was upon an elevation. He was magnificent from the outset; but when the decent sobrieties of the character began to give way, and the poison of self-love, in his conceit of the Countess's affection, gradually to work, you would have thought that the hero of La Mancha in person stood before you. How he went smiling to himself! with what ineffable carelessness would he twirl his gold chain! what a dream it was! you were infected with the illusion, and did not wish that it should be removed! you had no room for laughter! if an unseasonable reflection of morality obtruded itself, it was a deep sense of the pitiable infirmity of man's nature, that can lay him open to such frenzies — but, in truth, you rather admired than pitied the lunacy while it lasted — you felt that an hour of such mistake was worth an age with the eyes open. Who would not wish to live but for a day in the conceit of such a lady's love as Olivia? Why, the Duke would have given his principality but for a quarter of a minute, sleeping or waking, to have been so deluded. The man seemed to tread upon air, to taste manna, to walk with his head in the clouds, to mate Hyperion. O! shake not the castles of his pride — endure yet for a season, bright moments of confidence — "stand still, ye watches of the element," that Malvolio may be still in fancy fair Olivia's lord! — but fate and retribution say no — I hear the mischievous titter of Maria — the witty taunts of Sir Toby — the still more insupportable triumph of the foolish knight — the counterfeit Sir Topas is unmasked — and "thus the whirligig of time," as the true clown hath it, "brings in his revenges." I confess that I never saw the catastrophe of this character, while Bensley played it, without a kind of tragic interest. . . .

WILLIAM HAZLITT

Too Good-Natured for Comedy

TWELFTH NIGHT

THIS IS justly considered as one of the most delightful of Shakespear's comedies. It is full of sweetness and pleasantry. It is perhaps too good-natured for comedy. It has little satire, and no spleen. It aims at the ludicrous rather than the ridiculous. It makes us laugh at the follies of mankind, not despise them, and still less bear any ill-will towards them. Shakespear's comic genius resembles the bee rather in its power of extracting sweets from weeds or poisons, than in leaving a sting behind it. He gives the most amusing exaggeration of the prevailing foibles of his characters, but in a way that they themselves, instead of being offended at, would almost join in to humour; he rather contrives opportunities for them to shew themselves off in the happiest lights, than renders them contemptible in the perverse construction of the wit or malice of others. — There is a certain stage of society in which people become conscious of their peculiarities and absurdities, affect to disguise what they are, and set up pretensions to what they are not. This gives rise to a corresponding style of comedy, the object of which is to detect the disguises of self-love, and to make reprisals on these preposterous assumptions of vanity, by marking the contrast between the real and the affected character as severely as possible, and denying to those, who would impose on us for what they are not, even the merit which they have. This is the comedy of artificial life, of wit and satire, such as we see it in Congreve, Wycherly, Vanbrugh, etc. To this succeeds a state of society from which the same sort of affectation and pretence are banished by a greater knowledge of the world or by their successful exposure on the stage; and which by neutralising the materials of comic character, both natural and artificial, leaves no comedy at all — but *the sentimental*. Such is our modern comedy. There is a period in the progress of manners anterior to both these, in which the foibles and

Reprinted from *Characters of Shakespear's Plays*, 1817; in *The Complete Works of William Hazlitt*, ed. P. P. Howe, Vol. IV (1930), 313–15.

ndividuals are of nature's planting, not the growth of art or
which they are therefore unconscious of them themselves, or
_____ who knows them, if they can but have their whim out; and in
which, as there is not attempt at imposition, the spectators rather receive
pleasure from humouring the inclinations of the persons they laugh at,
than wish to give them pain by exposing their absurdity. This may be
called the comedy of nature, and it is the comedy which we generally
find in Shakespear. — Whether the analysis here given be just or not, the
spirit of his comedies is evidently quite distinct from that of the authors
above mentioned, as it is in its essence the same with that of Cervantes,
and also very frequently of Molière, though he was more systematic in
his extravagance than Shakespear. Shakespear's comedy is of a pastoral
and poetical cast. Folly is indigenous to the soil, and shoots out with
native, happy, unchecked luxuriance. Absurdity has every encouragement afforded it; and nonsense has room to flourish in. Nothing is
stunted by the churlish, icy hand of indifference or severity. The poet
runs riot in a conceit, and idolises a quibble. His whole object is to turn
the meanest or rudest objects to a pleasurable account. The relish which
he has of a pun, or of the quaint humour of a low character, does not
interfere with the delight with which he describes a beautiful image, or
the most refined love. . . . In a word, the best turn is given to every
thing, instead of the worst. There is a constant infusion of the romantic
and enthusiastic, in proportion as the characters are natural and sincere:
whereas, in the more artificial style of comedy, every thing gives way
to ridicule and indifference, there being nothing left but affectation on
one side, and incredulity on the other. — Much as we like Shakespear's
comedies, we cannot agree with Dr. Johnson that they are better than
his tragedies; nor do we like them half so well. If his inclination to
comedy sometimes led him to trifle with the seriousness of tragedy, the
poetical and impassioned passages are the best parts of his comedies.
The great and secret charm of *Twelfth Night* is the character of Viola.
Much as we like catches and cakes and ale, there is something that we
like better. We have a friendship for Sir Toby; we patronise Sir Andrew;
we have an understanding with the Clown, a sneaking kindness for
Maria and her rogueries, we feel a regard for Malvolio, and sympathise
with his gravity, his smiles, his cross garters, his yellow stockings, and
imprisonment in the stocks. But there is something that excites in us a
stronger feeling than all this — it is Viola's confession of her love. . . .

GEORGE BERNARD SHAW

Romantic Nonsense

A CREDO ON SHAKESPEARE

1. That the idolatry of Shakespear which prevails now existed in his own time, and got on the nerve of Ben Jonson.

2. That Shakespear was not an illiterate poaching laborer who came up to London to be a horseboy, but a gentleman with all the social pretensions of our higher *bourgeoisie.*

3. That Shakespear, when he became an actor, was not a rogue and a vagabond, but a member and part proprietor of a regular company, using, by permission, a nobleman's name as its patron, and holding itself as exclusively above the casual barnstormer as a Harley Street consultant holds himself above a man with a sarsaparilla stall.

4. That Shakespear's aim in business was to make money enough to acquire land in Stratford, and to retire as a country gentleman with a coat of arms and a good standing in the county; and that this was not the ambition of a *parvenu,* but the natural course for a member of the highly respectable, though temporarily impecunious, family of the Shakespears.

5. That Shakespear found that the only thing that paid in the theatre was romantic nonsense, and that when he was forced by this to produce one of the most effective samples of romantic nonsense in existence — a feat which he performed easily and well — he publicly disclaimed any responsibility for its pleasant and cheap falsehood by borrowing the story and throwing it in the face of the public with the phrase "As You Like It."

6. That when Shakespear used that phrase he meant exactly what he said, and that the phrase "What You Will," which he applied to *Twelfth*

The first selection is reprinted from *The Daily News of London,* April, 1905. The second selection consists of excerpts from an article in *The Saturday Review* of December 5, 1896; the third selection comes from *The Star* of April 18, 1890. A valuable and readily accessible collection is *Shaw on Shakespeare,* ed. Edwin Wilson, (New York: E. P. Dutton and Company, Inc., 1961). By permission of The Public Trustee and The Society of Authors, London. Title provided by the present editor.

Night, meaning "Call it what you please," is not, in Shakespearean or any other English, the equivalent of the perfectly unambiguous and penetratingly simple phrase "As You Like It."

7. That Shakespeare tried to make the public accept real studies of life and character in — for instance — *Measure for Measure* and *All's Well That Ends Well;* and that the public would not have them, and remains of the same mind still, preferring a fantastic sugar doll, like Rosalind, to such serious and dignified studies of women as Isabella and Helena.

8. That the people who spoil paper and waste ink by describing Rosalind as a perfect type of womanhood are the descendants of the same blockheads whom Shakespear, with the coat of arms and the lands in Warwickshire in view, had to please when he wrote plays as they liked them.

9. Not, as has been erroneously stated, that I could write a better play than *As You Like It,* but that I actually have written much better ones, and in fact, never wrote anything, and never intend to write anything, half so bad in matter. (In manner and art nobody can write better than Shakespear, because, carelessness apart, he did the thing as well as it can be done within the limits of human faculty.) . . .

11. That Shakespear's power lies in his enormous command of word music, which gives fascination to his most blackguardly repartees and sublimity to his hollowest platitudes.

12. That Shakespear's weakness lies in his complete deficiency in that highest sphere of thought, in which poetry embraces religion, philosophy, morality, and the bearing of these on communities, which is sociology. That his characters have no religion, no politics, no conscience, no hope, no convictions of any sort. That there are, as Ruskin pointed out, no heroes in Shakespear. That his test of the worth of life is the vulgar hedonic test and that since life cannot be justified by this or any other external test, Shakespear comes out of his reflective period a vulgar pessimist, oppressed with a logical demonstration that life is not worth living, and only surpassing Thackeray in respect to being fertile enough, instead of repeating *Vanitas vanitatum* at second hand to work the futile doctrine differently and better in such passages as "Out, out, brief candle."

FRANCIS FERGUSSON

Two Comedies

SHAKESPEARE'S COMEDY, both the plays called comedies and the comic passages in the rest of his work, is even harder to understand than his tragedy. The comic in general defies analysis: is there a definition of the laughable, even Bergson's, in which one can have much confidence? Some shrewd observations have been made on particular comedies or writers of comedy, but usually the critics merely prove that every real sense of humor, and even every comic effect, is unique. Molière comes as close as any master of comedy to having a stable point of view, an intelligible convention, and an infallible touch; but it is impossible to reduce all this to a formula. As for Shakespeare, his point of view shifts continually, he employs various conventions in his comedy, and there are many who find his touch far from infallible. Broadway reviewers, who think they know what makes the readers of *The New Yorker* laugh, and antiquarians, who think they know what made the Elizabethans laugh, tend to agree that Shakespeare's comedy is comic no more: here again they clasp hands, with a sophisticated wink, over the safely dead body of our heritage.

If one nevertheless does enjoy Shakespeare's humor, what is the best way to explore its range, learn its habits, assure oneself that one is really getting the point which Shakespeare intended? One method is to keep in mind the fact that Shakespeare wrote to be acted before an audience. One then reflects that laughter in the theater depends upon so many factors — the mood of the audience, what the author has led the audience, in advance, to expect; the rhythm of the performance as a whole; subtleties of timing, attitude, and the like — that it is to be understood and controlled only empirically. Directors and actors know this. Comedians, however talented, have to learn by trial and error how to make audiences laugh at them. Directors often have to experiment with a

From *The Human Image in Dramatic Literature*, Garden City, N.Y., 1957, Doubleday Anchor Books, pp. 144–158. Originally published in *The Sewanee Review*, LXII (1954). Copyright by *The Sewanee Review*. Reprinted by permission of the author and *The Sewanee Review*.

comic scene, cutting it, changing its timing or business, before they can see how it works. There is every reason to believe that Shakespeare, a practical theater man, worked that way. Starting with an old play or an old story, having in mind a certain company of actors, he wrote his plays in such a way as to control all the elements, and from their combination, before an audience, to get the intended effect of humor or pathos. Each of his comic effects is unique; emerging from the context of the whole acted play, it reflects his sure grasp of the action of *that* play, its comic as well as its pathetic aspects. His sense of humor apparently never sleeps; he reveals it, at will, by manipulating the theatrically perceptible elements which his story provides.

The most ambitious way to learn about Shakespeare's comedy would be to try to produce it. But the opportunity to do that is rare, and an actual production tests many things besides Shakespeare's dramaturgy, notably the skill and talent of the actors, and the moral and physical stamina of the hopeful director. It is an ordeal not to be lightly undertaken. A more practicable (as well as self-indulgent) method is to imagine the ideal performance as one reads the play — not, of course, in all its material details, but as a musician might "hear" a symphony as he read the score. Such a reading of Shakespeare's comedy would, I suppose, turn up much that is obvious; but it might have the value of a prolegomenon: a pedestrian preparation for understanding Shakespeare's comic genius.

The Comedy of Errors and *Much Ado About Nothing* are far from exhausting Shakespeare's comic resources. But they are very different from each other, and by thinking them over together, with an eye to their theatrical point, one may begin to sense the variety and scope of his comic repertoire.

I

Shakespeare took the main story of *The Comedy of Errors* from Plautus's *The Two Menaechmuses*. The basic situation is that of two brothers, identical twins, who were separated in childhood and find themselves by chance in the same city when they are grown; they are so identical that no one can tell them apart. It is very improbable that twins could be so similar that even the wife of one of them couldn't distinguish between them, but Plautus, and Shakespeare after him, calmly assume that identity, and they are right, for this initial absurdity sets the key of the farce to follow. The audience must accept the silly postulate at once; so it is warned to expect, not a fable purporting "truth," but a joke and a tall story.

I do not know why two people who are identical are laughable, but they are, and if they are not only the same height and age and weight, but walk and sit in the same way at the same time, the comic effect is stronger. And if there are more than two, we are still more pleased with them. This principle is well used in the Kaufman-Hart comedy, *Once in a Lifetime*, when twelve movie magnates, the identical Glogauer brothers, march onto the stage in a double-quick procession just before the second act curtain.

Shakespeare must have counted on this property of human identity, for when he devised *The Comedy of Errors* he provided Plautus's identical twins with servants who were also identical twins. He thus exaggerates Plautus's farcical exaggeration, and is enabled thereby to play many more variations than Plautus could on the plot which may be derived from the basic situation. This situation is the childishly simple one of mistaken identity: every scene in the play is an instance of it; every character in the play is always and only trying to straighten out such a mistake, which the audience always perfectly understands in advance. The most striking quality of this comedy — unique among Shakespeare's plays — is its perfect unity of action, plot and tone. As it quickly unrolls before us it gives the superficial impression of ceaseless movement, variety, and surprise. But that is a matter of great, but essentially mechanical, ingenuity: the play is built like a round, which delights a group of light-hearted singers by piling up and overlapping a single pattern.

It is true that the first scene, in which we see the twins' long-suffering father in trouble, and the last scene, in which father, mother, and the boys are reunited with happy tears, are different in tone from the body of the play: sentimental rather than farcical. But the first scene is a prologue, and the last scene not only brings the intrigue to its happy end, but also serves the essential purpose of changing the mood. Writers of farce have usually some trouble with the end of their fun. There is no inherent reason for halting the perpetual-motion machine of a good farcical plot; the arabesques of absurdity in *The Comedy of Errors* might continue indefinitely, or at least to the limits of the author's ingenuity and the audience's complacency. The plot is wound up neatly and naturally enough by the simple expedient of bringing both sets of twins together, but that is not enough: the postulate — or call it the attitude, or frame of mind — of farce must be broken through; the audience must be relaxed and dismissed in another mood. This may be accomplished in countless ways, but all who successfully devise farce for the theater feel the need of this final change of mood. I used to notice that the old burlesque shows at Minsky's recognized it instinctively. The traveling salesmen would be guffawing all evening at slapstick, broad jokes, and chorines with but three crucial rhinestones; but at the end the lights would soften, the music would slide from the hot, through the blue, to the frankly old-timy, and a gray-haired mamma or "mom" would take the center of the stage to gaze thoughtfully into the electric moonlight. So the patrons received the whole treatment, gently eased at last out of their farcical mood into something warmer, damper and homier.

There is one strand running through the whole *Comedy of Errors* which might seem, on a first reading, to break the mood of farce: the troubled adventures of Antipholus of Ephesus' long-suffering wife. She is so disturbed when the other Antipholus treats her strangely that one might think Shakespeare wanted us to share her tears and frustrations. She and her sister and her maid, and eventually her real husband's mistress, form a dreary female procession through the quick twists of the plot. But I believe that Shakespeare expected us to laugh at them also, and that, in performance, would be largely a matter of tempo. The film of a funeral, even, may be made laughable if it is run off at twice the proper speed, and if we saw the bewildered women running and dripping at the same time we should understand how they fit into the whole farcical scheme.

When Shakespeare wrote *The Comedy of Errors* he was aiming, with great accuracy, at the perennial popular theater. He demanded, therefore, very little of his audience. He does not expect us to be interested in the subtleties of character: the figures in this farce are labeled (as servant, man-about-town, wife or courtesan) just accurately enough to enable us to tell them apart. We are not called upon for much sympathy or imagination: in fact we must not try to see through these characters' eyes, or feel what they feel. It would ruin everything to take the wife's troubles, or Dromio's many beatings, at all seriously. All we have to do is grasp the broadly absurd situation, and follow the ingenious fugue of the plot. To get the point, nothing beyond mental alertness of an easy kind is required. The foolishness presented in this play is that of the incredible and arbitrary basic situation, not the ineluctable folly of mankind.

The play belongs in the stream of popular comedy, from Menander to Minsky; but it also shows an intelligence and control, on the part of the author, which is rare in any kind of play. It is much lighter and funnier than *The Two Menaechmuses*. This mastery is revealed, not so much in the language, though that is perfectly adequate to its modest purposes, as in the consistency with which its farcical limitations are accepted, and in the ingenuity of the plot. This plot really is built like the proverbial "Swiss watch": it is as absurdly neat as Leibniz's pre-established harmony. Comedy of this type, or taste—rationalistic, built on a Latin base—was to be more fully explored in the succeeding age of the Enlightenment, in the innumerable comedies which lighted the theaters of Europe from Molière through Mozart. But Shakespeare was developing in a different direction, not toward the univocal perfection of the geometric diagram, but toward the harmonizing of complementary perspectives; not toward further ingenuity, but toward deeper insight.

The Comedy of Errors, like other comedies of that taste, is so clear that it *ought* to be reducible to a formula. Molière's comedies often strike us in the same way. Certainly one can find in them many standard and publicly available devices, whether of plotting, attitude, or conventional characterization. Without that heritage I do not suppose Shakespeare could, at so early an age, have written anything so easy and assured. Yet he uses it for his own purposes, like a good cook who first learns and then forgets the basic recipes, or a dress designer who assumes the clichés of fashion only to go beyond them to something not quite predictable. Only Shakespeare could derive The Comedy of Errors from Plautus, and only he could proceed from that simple fun to the enigmatic humor of his maturity.

II

When Shakespeare wrote Much Ado About Nothing he had lost none of his skill as a maker of plots; on the contrary, he had attained further mastery in the ten years or more since the writing of The Comedy of Errors. There are three main narrative-lines: that of Claudio, Hero, and the wicked Don John; the connected story of Dogberry and the Watch; and the contrasting story of Beatrice and Benedick, all interwoven with clarity and apparent ease. But in this play Shakespeare uses the plot for a further and deeper end. Each of the three narrative-lines has its own humor, and by the interplay of the three a more general vision of man as laughable is suggested: a vision which is at once comic and poetic.

The story of young Claudio and Hero caught in Don John's wicked schemes was Shakespeare's starting point, and the somewhat casual framework of the plot of the whole play. He had read this story in Bandello's version, Timbreo di Cardona, the story of a girl unjustly accused of adultery. This tale, though it ends happily, is not very funny in itself, and Shakespeare does not so much avoid its painful and pathetic aspects as absorb them in his more detached comic vision. The scene in the church, when poor Hero is wrongly accused and her father Leonato loudly laments, may be played for a "tragic" effect, but that I think would not be quite right. The audience knows that it is all a mistake, and it is by that time accustomed to smile at Claudio, an absurdly solemn victim of young love's egoism. When he first appears he tries to tell the Duke what the Duke knew already: his all-important love for Hero. He glumly decides that the Duke, wooing Hero in his behalf, has stolen her, and so is wrong again. Beatrice labels him for us:

"glum as an orange, and something of that jealous complexion." His false accusation is his third mistake: we must sympathize, but at the same time smile, at this final instance of his foolishness. The whole Claudio-Hero story is comic in itself and in its own way, but to understand what Shakespeare meant by it it is necessary to think of it in relation to the two other stories which unfold in alternation with it.

Dogberry and the Watch are closely connected with the Claudio story, which requires someone to uncover Don John's plot, but Shakespeare developed this element into a farcical sequence with its own tone and interest. At the same time he uses it to lighten the catastrophe at Hero's wedding, and the character of Don John: we cannot take a villain seriously who can be apprehended by Dogberry. Dogberry is not suffering the delusions of young love, like Claudio, but those of vanity and uncontrollable verbosity. His efforts to find his way, with lanterns, through the darkness of the night and the more impenetrable darkness of his wits, forms an ironic parallel to the groping of the young lovers through their mists of feeling. Dogberry also has his version of the underlying mood of the play — that of a leisurely and joyful ease, such as we attribute to Eden or the Golden Age. In Dogberry this infatuated leisureliness, this delusion that nothing terrible can really happen, takes the form of interminable verbalizing while the evil plot hatches and the villains lurk uncaught.

The story of Beatrice and Benedick's self-tormented love affair is entirely Shakespeare's creation. He seems to have felt the need of that pair's intelligence and agility to ventilate Claudio and Hero. We should tire quickly of Claudio's total submersion in love if Benedick were not there, pretending to be too intelligent for that. Hero, who can only sigh and blush, would be too soggy without Beatrice, who can only make sharp remarks, pull pigtails, and stick her tongue out at the boys. But the two contrasting stories together suggest a vision of early infatuation — provided we don't take Shakespeare's characters more seriously than he intended — which is both deeper and more comic than the victims themselves can know.

Beatrice and Benedick are notoriously hard to act on the modern stage, especially in the first two acts, where they indulge in so many quibbles and conceits in the taste of their times. There is no use trying to make the verbal jokes funny; but I am not sure that Shakespeare himself took them seriously as jokes. I once had the pleasure of seeing John Gielgud and Pamela Brown act several of the Beatrice-Benedick scenes. They "threw away" the words, or even, at moments, made fun of their far-fetched elaboration, and by this means focused their audience's attention on the noble, silly, intelligent and bewildered *relation* of the two — a relation as agile, musical, and deeply comic as that of

Congreve's reluctant lovers, Mirabel and Millamant. I feel sure that this approach to the play is right: its surfaces, its literal words, characters and events, are not to be taken seriously: the point is in the music of unseen motivation, in the fact that it *is* unseen by the characters themselves — and that all the fun and folly plays against a background of mystery.

The main Claudio-Hero-Don John intrigue is also not to be taken too seriously, as though it were the point of the play: Shakespeare gets it under way casually, after the underlying mood of the play as a whole, and its "action" of elaborate play, or leisurely enjoyment, has been firmly established. The opening scene, in which Leonato's household prepares to celebrate the return of the Duke, Benedick and Claudio from their comic-opera war, tells us what the play is really about: it is a festive occasion, a celebration of a certain evanescent but recurrent human experience. The experience is real in its way, all may recognize it, but under its spell everything the characters do is much ado about nothing. The progress of the underlying action of the play as a whole is therefore marked by a series of somewhat dreamy and deluded festive occasions. The first of these is Leonato's masked ball, in Act II, a visible and musical image of the action. Then comes Dogberry's nocturnal and incomprehensible charge to the Watch: a farcical version of the theme. The fourth act consists chiefly of the marriage which turns out to be no marriage at all, but a bad dream. In the fifth act there is Claudio's funeral tribute to Hero, by night, at her supposed tomb; but this is a funeral which is no funeral, corresponding to the marriage which was no marriage. After that pathetic and comic expiatory rite, daylight returns, the torches are put out, and we are ready for the real and double marriage, in daylight, with the ladies unmasked at last, which ends the play in dance and song.

We are just beginning to understand the technical value of the "ceremonious occasion" as an element of plot, though it has been used in countless ways from Aristophanes to Henry James. When people assemble for a ceremonious occasion (whether it be the festival of Dionysos or one of James's thorny tea parties) they must abate, or conceal, their purely individual purposes, and recognize the common concern which brings them together. A dramatist may use the festive occasion, therefore, to shift his audience's attention from the detail of the literal intrigue to some general plight which all more or less unwittingly share. All are social and political animals; all must suffer spring, mating, and death. Ceremonious occasions are especially useful to dramatists who are seeking poetry, which, as Aristotle remarked, is concerned with something more general than the particular facts, the unique events, of human life. The point — the comic point — of *Much*

Ado — is poetic in that sense, and hence it is the festive ensemble scenes which most clearly adumbrate the basic vision of the play. In this respect the plot of *Much Ado* contrasts sharply with that of *The Comedy of Errors*. The point of that play lies precisely in the unique situation of mistaken identity, and in the strings of absurd events which quickly follow from it. An "occasion" of any kind would break the tight concatenation of *contretemps;* and that Shakespeare is careful to avoid doing until he is ready to end the whole play.

One might say that *Much Ado* presents a comic vision of mankind which is also poetic, while the purpose of *The Comedy of Errors* is closer to that of the professional vaudevillian, who gauges his success by clocking the laughs: the provoking of thoughtless mirth, an almost reflex response. The difference between the two plays is clearest, perhaps, when one reflects that both are concerned with mistaken identity, but in *The Comedy of Errors* the mistake is simply a mistake in fact, while in *Much Ado* it is a failure of insight, or rather many failures of different kinds by the different characters.

Shakespeare accomplishes the *dénouement* of *The Comedy of Errors* in one swift scene. It is not difficult to correct an error in fact: it may be done instantly by providing the right fact: and as soon as both pairs of twins are on stage together, the error is gone. But correcting a failure of insight is a most delicate and mysterious process, which Shakespeare suggests, in *Much Ado,* in countless ways: through the symbolism of masks, night, and verbal ambiguities, and in peripeteias of his three variously comic subplots.

The farcical efforts of Dogberry and Verges never deviate into enlightenment. They learn as little as the characters in *The Comedy of Errors:* but, like them, they do stumble eventually upon the right fact: they manage to apprehend the villains and convey that fact to Leonato.

Claudio, with his dark fumes of love, has a long way to go before he can see anything real. After his false wedding Shakespeare puts him through a false and painful challenge from his best friend, Benedick, and then the mocking (but touching) mummery of his visit to Hero's empty tomb. Even then the audience learns more from Claudio's masquerade-like progress through the maze than he does himself.

Beatrice and Benedick come the closest, of all the characters, to grasping the whole scope of the comic vision which the play slowly unfolds. But even after their friends have tried to kid them out of their frightened vanity during the first three acts, it takes most of the fourth and fifth acts, where all the painful things occur, to bring them to conscious acceptance of their absurd selves, each other, and their love. It is the fiasco of Claudio's first attempt at marriage which marks the crucial turn in their relationship:

BENEDICK: Lady Beatrice, have you wept all this while?
BEATRICE: Yea, and I will weep a while longer.

and a little later:

BENEDICK: I do love nothing in the world so well as you. Is not that strange?
BEATRICE: As strange as the thing I know not. It were as possible for me to
to say I love nothing so well as you; but believe me not; and yet I lie
not; I confess nothing. . . .

In this exchange the love-warmed final scene of the play is foreshadowed,
but the misfortunes of Claudio and Hero, which here bring Beatrice and
Benedick near together, immediately carry them apart again. Benedick
has to challenge Claudio, and that boy's delusions have to be repented
and dispelled, before Beatrice and Benedick can trust their intuition of
love, or accept it fully and in good conscience. I do not attempt to
follow the subtle shifts in their relationship which Shakespeare suggests,
in a few quick, sure strokes, during the fifth act. But it is Beatrice and
Benedick who dominate the final scene:

BENEDICK: Soft and fair, Friar. Which is Beatrice?
BEA. (unmasking): I answer to that name. What is your will?
BEN.: Do not you love me?
BEA.: Why no, no more than reason.
BEN.: Why then, your uncle and the Prince and Claudio have been
deceived; they swore you did.
BEA.: Do not you love me?
BEN.: Troth no, no more than reason.
BEA.: Why then my cousin, Margaret, and Ursula are much deceived, for
they did swear you did.

(Claudio and Hero produce love letters from Benedick and Beatrice to each
other)

BEN.: A miracle! here's our own hands against our hearts. Come, I will
have thee; but, by this light, I take thee for pity.
BEA.: I would not deny you, but by this good day I yield upon great
persuasion, and partly to save your life, for I was told you were in a
consumption.
BEN.: Peace; I will stop your mouth.

In this scene the main contrasting themes of the play are brought
together, and very lightly and quickly resolved: marriage true and false,
masking and unmasking, the delusion and truth of youthful love. The
harmonies may all be heard in Beatrice's and Benedick's words. The
exchange is in prose, but (like the prose of Leonato's masked ball) it has

a rhythm and a varied symmetry suggesting the formality of a dance figure. The key words — love, reason, day, light, pity, peace — make music both for the ear and for the understanding as they echo back and forth, deepening in meaning with each new context. The effect of the scene as a whole is epitomized in Beatrice's and Benedick's heavenly double-take: their foolish idiosyncrasy is clear, but some joyful flood of acceptance and understanding frees them, for the moment, and lifts them beyond it. Is this effect "comic"? I do not know; I think it is intended to bring a smile, not for the windup of this little plot, but for the precarious human condition.

When one reads *Much Ado* in the security of one's own room, indulging in daydreams of an ideal performance, it is possible to forget the practical and critical problems which surround the question of the play's viability in our time. But it must be admitted that high school productions are likely to be terribly embarrassing, and I do not even like to think of the play's pathetic vulnerability on Times Square. The play demands much from its performers, almost as much as Chekhov does. It demands a great deal from its audience: a leisurely and contemplative detachment which seems too costly in our hustled age. Perhaps Shakespeare should be blamed for all this: if *Much Ado* does not easily convince us on the contemporary stage, perhaps we should conclude, as Eliot once concluded of *Hamlet,* that it is an artistic failure. But on that principle we should have to rule out a great deal of Shakespeare. It was his habit, not only in *Hamlet* and *Much Ado,* but in many other plays, to indicate, rather than explicitly to present, his central theme; and to leave it to his performers and his audience to find it behind the varied episodes, characters, and modes of language which are literally presented. Everything which Shakespeare meant by *The Comedy of Errors* is immediately perceptible; the comic vision of *Much Ado* will only appear, like the faces which Dante saw in the milky substance of the moon, slowly, and as we learn to trust the fact that it is really there.

A. P. ROSSITER

Much Ado about Nothing

THE PLAY'S date (1598 seems secure)[1] invites one of two general approaches to interpretation. *Either* this is all trivial, however clever: the author is totally disengaged throughout, and we are foolish to look for anything in any way deep, ourselves solemnly making ado about nothing; *or* it is a brilliantly superficial and deliberately *limited* "Italian" love-fantasia on the theme of deception by appearances (all sorts of deceptions, by several sorts of appearances): and we remember that seeming and being will provide plots in very different tones from this, in the plays that Shakespeare goes on to write in 1599 and later. . . .

. . . Although it remains possible that the 1598 composition may have been from an earlier draft (perhaps a mere sketch); and true that writing of distinguishably different sorts is juxtaposed in it, together with the uncertainties and dead-ends which result from quick composition. Detective-story consistency, and the elimination of all redundancies and contradictions, are not to be expected of an Elizabethan and especially not of a dramatist.[2] In short, the slight internal contradictions seen on reading do not signify (if Shakespeare saw them); and do not matter much, if we do. The "old" matter (if it was old) suited certain contrasts which Shakespeare wanted to draw around 1598, and gave the "main" plot the right lack of emphasis for the task in hand. There is no reason to doubt that the emphasis on Benedick and Beatrice is

"Much Ado about Nothing" by A. P. Rossiter, from *Angel with Horns* by A. P. Rossiter, edited by Graham Storey, © by Longmans, Green & Co., Ltd. 1961; reprinted with the permission of Theatre Arts Books, New York. Minor deletions have been authorized by Theatre Arts Books.

[1] Because (*a*) Meres would have mentioned it, had it been acted by 1597; and he does not. (*b*) in Q (1600) Dogberry and Verges are described in speech-headings as Kempe and Cowley; and Kempe left the Company during 1599 (*c*) Jonson's *Everyman in his Humour* (performed 1598) had popularized the humour of Humours; and the uses of it in *Much Ado,* though the word was not at all new, certainly sound like easy allusions to a newly fashionable interest in it.

[2] The question, for example, of how Beatrice came not to sleep with Hero on the fatal pre-marital night, is simply improper in terms of stage-convention. Dramatists would emphasize seeming guilt in such ways, without realizing that another convention would want to have the answers to "Why?", "Where was she?", etc.

deliberate, whether he worked from a draft, a sketch, or in some other way. Nor, I think, can we fail to observe that in the "main" plot *some* passages of a tone too disturbed or disturbing for the "Old Play," or for early work, "arrived" in the course of writing out, because there were already in his mind feelings and reflections on, say, "what men daily do, not knowing what they do": feelings which were, after 1598, to lead his work towards tragi-comedy (of a sort that this play is *not*).

Deception by appearances in *love* is patently what most of *Much Ado* is "about." As Hero puts it:

> Of this matter
> Is little Cupid's crafty arrow made,
> That only wounds by hearsay ... (III. i. 21–3)

Cupid is not responsible for calumny; but "hearsay" is a main force in both love-plots: each is about its effects on proud, self-willed, self-centred and self-admiring creatures, whose comedy is at bottom that of imperfect self-knowledge, which leads them on to fool themselves. Is it exaggeration to bring even Dogberry into this pattern? to point to his manifest self-admiration ("a fellow that hath had losses; and one that hath two gowns, and everything handsome about him"), and to hint that the little arrow that wounds *him* "by hearsay" is magnificent language and "wit"? Are not words and wisdom his Cupids? No doubt that stretches "love" too far. But self-love is a common term to all three of the splendid comedians of the piece.

The play's wit has been justly praised and is worth some examination in detail. It is of several distinguishable sorts: the simpler important only in so far as contributing to the cumulative effect, one of impetuous exuberance, a kind of competitive vitality, expressing itself in quick manipulations of language. The Messinians have dancing minds, and make words dance or caper to their unpremeditated tunes. At its simplest level, it is mere quibble: where A has used a word capable of two meanings in different contexts, and B shows his awareness of both, by displacing it. This may be no more than a conventional game, "comic wit degenerating into clenches,"[3] and though editors explain them, "the mind," as Johnson says, "is refrigerated by interruption." *Much Ado* suffers but little from this. It may, again, be an elaboration of that: when A and B are the same person, as when Beatrice "takes herself up" on Claudio: "The Count is neither sad, nor sick, nor merry, nor well; but civil count — civil as an orange, and something of that jealous complexion." (II. i. 262–4.) That is exactly at the point where mere verbal cleverness, non-significant quibble, passes over into relevant wit: evoca-

[3] Dryden: *Essay of Dramatic Poesy.*

tive here either of Beatrice's vitality (the "character" view), or of the exuberant quality of lively minds which strike fire by scoring off each other: the quality I called *competitive* vitality, as of a "college of wit-crackers."

In the wit-game Benedick and Beatrice rightly regard themselves as "seeded" players. Beatrice makes this clear in the scene in Hero's apartment before the wedding (III. iv.), when Margaret scores off her for once. Shown Hero's new gloves, she is not interested (her mind is bothered with Benedick), and unguardedly pretends to have a cold:

> I am stuff'd, cousin, I cannot smell.
> MARGARET: A maid and stuff'd! There's goodly catching of cold.
> BEATRICE: O, God help me! God help me! How long have you profess'd apprehension?

("Since when have you been a wit-cracker in this line?" — which Beatrice regards, with good reason, as her own.) Beatrice gets more of her own medicine later, over the prescription of "Carduus Benedictus": here the wit is both verbal and something more — we might call it the wit of situation. No precise *double-entendre* is made; but Beatrice's state of mind is such that she feels (like Benedick before her) "there's a double meaning in that"; and she lays herself open to another laugh by again using the wrong word:

> Benedictus! why Benedictus? You have some moral in this "Benedictus."
> MARGARET: Moral? No, by my troth, I have no moral meaning.

It is a notable point in Shakespeare's contrivance that he gives both wits their off-day, as soon as love has disturbed their freedom.

As a rule, bawdy quibble outlives its contemporaries—simply because of "human nature"; or because the fundamental situation is practically constant. In this play, jesting about sex is apposite: its subjects are sex-opposition, wooing, wedding, wiving (with due attention to the dangers of the last in making sport of a man). The audience certainly laughed at Benedick's "Well, a horn for my money, when all's done" (II. iii. 56), the second time they saw the play. It becomes comic dramatic irony, if you read Elizabethanly. Yet, quite often, I see no great gain by doing so. There is something pathetic in the detailed scholarship which laboriously strives to conjure from its grave every ghost of an expired laugh.[4] "Lighthearted bawdry" has its point in *Much Ado* (as in Mercutio); but only the best of points can stand heavy-handed annotation. Much of it turns on obsolete phrases: the fuse of

---

[4] The smutty puns, for example, humourlessly expounded by Kökeritz in *Shakespeare's Pronunciation,* are often so far-fetched as to be linguistically dubious and not worth the carriage.

the whole firework has to be replaced with a dry note; and the verbal transaction, by losing all its speed, loses nearly all its crack. Quibble in slow-motion ceases to be witty. None the less, by noticing or examining the dexterities of verbal switch required, we are speeded up to a better awareness of the Elizabethan manipulations of language; and, at the same time, made more conscious of the vitality evoked individually by characters, and cumulatively by quibble, pun and jest together.

Shakespeare's wit in devising the linguistic mishaps and semantic excesses of Dogberry is the other side to the flat and despised "mere quibble." Dogberry exaggerates, by accident and in self-satisfied ignorance, the processes by which the true wits divert the meanings of words deliberately, knowingly, and with pride in their craft. But the one is the antithesis to the other; and both sides could be told, "Thou hast frighted the word out of his right sense, so forcible is thy wit" (Benedick to Beatrice, v. ii. 48). Wit and nitwit share a common obsessive delight in the wonders of words. This is largely what makes Dogberry the apposite farce-fool for a play in which all three plots turn on understandings and misunderstandings: quite apart from his being a marvel of the official numbskull's capacity to make extreme ado about genuine nothing.

But has the "Malaprop" had its day? It took the stage in *Woodstock* (? 1594), was cornered by Sheridan, survived to Dickens. It is perhaps funniest in hierarchical societies, where clever and witty management (or mismanagement) of language distinguishes the *élite;* and aping this makes the linguistic lower orders flatteringly absurd. My impression is that Malaprops are only comic nowadays to over-language-conscious schoolmasters; or, of course, when bawdily Dogburian: when the right idea comes out in very much the wrong word. But, unless I mistake, Dogberry's skids are never improper. Impropriety in this play is the privilege of the educated.

The wit that does *not* turn on word-play is best shown by examples. Essentially it is the exuberance which leaps beyond expectation in "improving the occasion." Not only Benedick and Beatrice have this hyperbolic comic inventiveness: the former his strokes of Falstaffian invention, the latter her alarming opportunism (she is likely to score suddenly off anyone, at any time). The qualities of swiftness and unexpectedness are just as neatly shown by old Leonato's perfectly timed shot at Benedick. Don Pedro asks if Hero is Leonato's daughter. "Her mother hath many times told me so," is the conventional formula in reply. "Were you in doubt, sir, that you ask'd her?" asks Benedick. "Signior Benedick, no; for then were you a child" (a palpable hit). They appear equally in Beatrice's magnificent impertinence to Don Pedro. he must cry "Heigh ho for a husband!" —

> Don Pedro: Lady Beatrice, I will get you one.
> Beatrice: I would rather have one of your father's getting. . . .

And the quality of "comic inventiveness" is shown immediately after, when he teasingly offers himself, and she says she will not have him unless she can have another for working-days: he is so costly she would have to keep him for best.

Both quickness of repartee and comic inventiveness (hyperbolic feats of exaggeration and elaboration) are intrinsic to the attitudes of self-dramatization upon which the comedy of character depends. Energy is delight and accomplished dexterity a pleasure to watch. Benedick and Beatrice have both: all the more because they are playing a part before themselves, and playing it high in an infectious sort of daring: figures of pride, which is at once humanly splendid, and "goes before a fall." There is no need to repeat what others have said of their proud hearts as a source of misogamy, because marriage means submission and commonplaceness. Benedick shows a more delicately amusing self-conceit than this in, for example, the admirable lines (v. ii. 63ff.), where the two mock-solemnly agree (a) that they are too wise to woo peaceably, and (b) that not one wise man among twenty will praise himself. Benedick then hits the high note impeccably with "Therefore is it most expedient for the wise, if Don Worm, his conscience, find no impediment to the contrary, to be the trumpet of his own virtues, as I am to myself" — a pause, to let the conceit of it shock all modest minds; then he goes one better — "So much for praising myself, who, I myself will bear witness, is praiseworthy." Here he is playing the Falstaffian game of carrying outrageousness as far as it will go. The *other* side of this self-conceit is in ii. iii. 200 ff., his solemn resolutions to profit morally by what he has overheard on his character: "I must not seem proud; happy are they that hear their detractions and can put them to mending"; and the heroic resolve to make the supreme sacrifice: "No; the world must be peopled." There, he is magnificently *absurd*, and totally unaware of himself. I stress the point to bring out the unappreciated fact that the common distinction between persons we laugh *at* and those we laugh *with* is too naïve and crude, at any rate for Shakespeare. Benedick's subsequent efforts to extract a double meaning from two snubbing sentences of Beatrice's repeat this vista of ingenious absurdity. Besides being excellent comedy of mistaken meanings, the last speech in ii. iii. is a perfect miniature sample of the love-humour racing a man past himself: "I will go get her picture." (*Exit*)

It may seem a wantonly paradoxical view, in so verbally brilliant a piece, but I would contend that some of the wittiest work is to be found in the interrelations and inter-inanimations of the plots. Of the three, the one that takes attention foremost is technically a sub-plot. We hardly notice that it gets going before the "main" plot, but Beatrice is "at" Benedick before Claudio appears; and this sex-antagonism in a fencing match between experts with sharp words is musically "the first subject." The comedy of this Benedick and Beatrice plot is not the simple, sentimental indulgence of the "boy meets girl" pattern, although that is included; rather it lies in the entertaining, good-natured, critically aware contemplation of the bents in human nature shown in (*a*) their antagonism (their incapacity to leave one another alone); (*b*) their deception by contrived intrigue; (*c*) the revelations which spring from this, under the pressure of circumstances (that arise from the main plot): leading to (*d*) reversal of all their first positions. The audience is always in a slightly superior position, *not* identifying itself with either of them, though sympathetic. When all the analysers have anatomized, and perhaps reconstructed Benedick and Beatrice, they remain "just representations of general nature," and hence, as Johnson says, "please many and please long."

If I were to answer in a word what the Benedick and Beatrice plot turns on, I should say *misprision*. Benedick and Beatrice misapprehend both each other *and* themselves: each misprizes the other sex, and misapprehends the possibility of a complete agreement between them, as individuals, on what causes that misprision: love of freedom and a superior conceit of themselves as "wise" where others are fools; as "free" and untied; and as having a right to enjoy kicking over other people's traces. They fancy they are quite different *from*, and quite indifferent *to* each other. Indifferent they are not; and the audience is "superior" in seeing their humours *as* humours; and in being aware that the opposite to love (as passionate, obsessive interest) is not hate (another passionate interest), but cool or unnoting indifference. How little Beatrice's "disdain" for Benedick is truly disdainful is shown in her immediately thinking of him as a measure for Don John (ii. i. 6 ff).

Because the mind of each runs on the other, they can both be simply gulled by hearsay; provided that it is overheard and includes the sort of freedom of comment we all use on absent friends: mildly malicious in tone, unspiteful in intent, and near enough true on their recognizable oddities and shortcomings. The overhearers, for all their sharpness of wit, know that the *comments* have some truth, and naturally accept the rest as also true.[5] Thus the introduction of love-thoughts into both results from a species of misapprehension. They take the *sense* of the words, but totally fail to apprehend their *intention*. The two gulling scenes belong to the comedy of advertisement. Even the advertisers' nice touches

[5] cf. Aristotle on lying, *Poetics*, 24. 9: "Homer more than any other has taught the rest of us the art of telling lies in the right way. I mean the use of a fallacy," *et seq*.

of flattery are not lacking. The criticism is spiced with proper appreciation, as when Don Pedro hints — a very subtle inducement — that he would quite like to have Beatrice himself.

That the "main" plot of Hero and Claudio turns on misapprehension leading to the misprision of violent disprizing, is too obvious to need commentary: but much of the play's total effect hangs on the structural mainness of this plot being displaced. As in Mannerist pictures sometimes, the emphasis is made to fall on what appears structurally to be a corner. This displaced emphasis helps to maintain the sense that the "Ado" is about "Nothing" (it is only through the distortion that reading gives, that much attention is given to the "character" of Claudio).

But though the misapprehension from judging by appearances is quite obvious, it is easy to overlook the incidental touches by which the theme of false report, misunderstanding and jumping to conclusions is strengthened. Not logically strengthened: the "incidents" are not necessary to the *story*; but the whole sub-episode of the proxy wooing does chime in cleverly with what is to follow. Don Pedro agrees to woo Hero; *immediately* Leonato's "good sharp fellow" overhears and misreports (I. ii. 5 ff.); the correct report gets into the wrong ears, Borachio's; he tells Don John, who straightaway uses it maliciously on Claudio (pretending to think him Benedick behind the masque-vizor). And Claudio at once anticipates his later violent and self-regarding impetuosity by assuming that Don Pedro *has* cheated him of Hero. Call this "atmosphere," if you like; say, perhaps, that Messina is no place to trust any man's word; whatever you say, it strengthens the theme; and the ready *and perhaps drastic* misapprehensions of quick and apprehensive minds appear as of major importance in the play, as a play and not as a merely logical story.

I say "perhaps drastic" to suggest how the matter of this part is balanced neatly on a tonal frontier: not between comedy and tragedy, but between comedy and tragi-comedy. Hence the "limited" of my description of the play at the beginning: the drastic possibilities are so lightly touched that there is a sense of withholding — as if the author, in another mood, could give these incidents quite another tone: but not now; not yet. This feeling is most evident in the Church-scene, which is *not* tragic. T. W. Craik's line[6] here is mainly sound; and his interpretation that *all* the passions are presented to be viewed with comic detachment is preferable to the conventional explanation, that "the audience is throughout in the know," etc.[7]

Without striving to make too much of it, the dance in II. i. is beautifully apposite. The couples walk their round, two by two, all masked; and all are using words to back the disguise of false faces with trivial deceit. The

6 In *Scrutiny*, xix (1953).
7 So is the audience in *Othello*, for what that is worth!

play-acted defamation of Hero, by means of a false dress on the wrong woman and names used falsely, is exactly parallel. In both, the truth is *behind* the looks and words. The *bal masqué* is only a game of seeming; yet it is a most apt symbol of the whole. The vizor is half deceit, half no deceit: you can never be sure. Believe it, and you make ado about what is nothing. And in the social order and shared delight of the dance — all moving to the controlling rhythm, in their appointed patterns — there is too the emblem of the harmony in which all will conclude: as the play does, with another dance, all the vizors laid aside. The real play is not ended with "Strike up, pipers." The very moment of II. i., where all the main misapprehensions started, is repeated and completed; and even the professed misogamists are dancing to the same tune. It is as neat and pretty as "Sigh no more, ladies, sigh no more."

The third plot — Dogberry, Verges, the Watch — though mainly Dogberry, is not a mere farcical variety-turn: there *is* a thread of connected episode. The Watch overhear Borachio's scheme and hear it correctly enough (their invention of a thief named "Deformed" is a nice touch: he has arrived at official constabulary existence by the end). They only overhear because they carry out Dogberry's ridiculous orders and make the policeman's lot a not-unhappy one by, as far as possible, doing nothing whatever. Despite their superb stupidity they do disentangle the plot: though only because, Don John having fled, Borachio tells everything, and gives them the game hands down. This is very natural and well-managed. For had Borachio set out to bluff, the Watch would have been utterly bamboozled in no time. *Superb* stupidity, however, belongs more rightly to Dogberry alone. One side of him is his art of "comprehending vagrom" *words:* there a more "senseless and fit man" could not be found. But this is not the whole of him; though a part entirely harmonious with the whole. Dogberry is a perfect instance of the comic mirth which Plato explained in *Philebus:* "mirth," he says, "is generally evoked by the sight of self-ignorance or self-conceit, as when a man fancies himself richer, more handsome, more virtuous or wiser than he really is; and this mirth must be present in one who is powerless to inflict hurt on others, otherwise he would cease to be a source of mirth and become a source of danger instead."[8] As a *real* official Dogberry would be a terror. Conceited ignorance and vast self-importance in local government officers is — and was, in the time of Elizabeth — as good a joke in fiction as a very bad joke in fact.

But misprision and misapprehension are present here too, in a different guise. The incomprehension of the stupid ass is a limiting case of failure to apprehend; and over and above his miscomprehensions of

[8] *Philebus,* 48–9 (summarized).

language, Dogberry's own view of Dogberry is a vast misprision. To himself a superb creature, a wise fellow, as pretty a piece of flesh as any in Messina, he is superbly asinine in the Messina of wit and word-play. Yet, while apparently an *opposite* to the wit-crackers, he is also a parallel: in that pride of self-opinion and a nice appreciation of one's own wisdom and cleverness is as much theirs as his. There is no caustic correction of self-love in Benedick or Beatrice. But the parallel gives another common term, showing on analysis how the three plots have their implicit correspondences, how they genuinely belong together.

"Nothing can permanently please, which does not contain in itself the reason why it is so, and not otherwise." I have been trying to probe down to the nervous system of those interrelations which *Much Ado* contains within itself, and which give it, as comedy, the poetic unity Coleridge there demands. I find a complex harmony of interdependent themes, some parallels, some direct oppositions; and it seems to me that misapprehensions, misprisions, misunderstandings, misinterpretations and misapplications are the best names for what the comedy *as a whole* is "about." The misapprehensions of language are one side of the play; those of human beings and states of affairs the other. At root the two are one; and both you can regard with Dogberry's formula for obdurate drunks: "You may say they are not the men you took them for." A step or stage beyond this, and what a different pattern of seemings might result: where neither looks nor words are to be trusted, but everything distrusted. . . . But *Much Ado* touches that for only a moment, and that unsymptomatic of the whole; for a few lines of Claudio's in the Church-scene. They only point to what *might* be thought and felt: in the real tragi-comedies it *will* be. Yet even in *Much Ado,* all appearances *are* equivocal.

Before leaving the plots, mark how deftly they are intertwined. Benedick and Beatrice misapprehend themselves and misprize each other. Claudio's contrived misprision of Hero, the result of intrigue, is finally dissipated by the *coup* of the Watch, which reduces all the ado to nothing. But at its zenith this same disprizing is the catalyst which liquidates the mutual misprisions of Benedick and Beatrice in the Church-scene. But the reactions to that scene (the confessions of love and Beatrice's implicit admission that she needs a man — to "kill Claudio") only occur because Benedick and Beatrice have been prepared to "apprehend": prepared by intrigue, which, like Don John's is dependent on hearsay and overhearing, taking appearances at their face-value, and being led or misled by words.[9]

Words I must stress, because Dogberry is no essential part of this

---

9 cf. the fusing of plot with plot in *The Miller's Tale.*

intertwining as I have summarized it. I suppose you could formulate it all again by saying that the controlling theme might be styled "mistaken identities"; for, in their pride or conceit, all the principals in some degree mistake themselves: as they mistake or wrongly take situations, and mistake or wrongly take words, on purpose and wittily or accidentally and absurdly. Leonato and Antonio, the two old men lashing themselves back into a youthful fury, and threatening duels, equally mistake themselves: they are pathetic and laughable at once. And, in a way, they reflect on Benedick's sternly assuming the role of truculent executioner to Claudio — and having a comical difficulty in maintaining the part. This is a good example of Shakespeare's detachment in this play: of the amused distance at which his creations should be held, if we are to take *Much Ado* as an artistic whole.

Despite Coleridge's too often quoted comment, "The interest in the plot is always in fact on account of the characters, not vice versa, as in almost all other writers; the plot is a mere canvas and no more,"[10] I still think that plot (in a deeper sense than "story") is here even more important. His implied contention that the "interest" in the main plot is "on account of the characters" (Hero and Claudio, chiefly; and I suppose Don John) seems to me simply untrue. Against Coleridge and his echoers we might set Jonson, putting Aristotelian principle in his own words, and answering the question "What is a Poet?": "A poet . . . is a maker, or a feigner: his art, an art of imitation or feigning; expressing the life of man in fit measure, numbers, and harmony. . . . Hence he is called a poet, not he which writeth in measure only, but that feigneth and formeth a fable, and writes things like the truth. For the fable and fiction is, at it were, the form and soul of any poetical work or poem."[11] In a later note, "the very fiction itself," he says, is "the reason or form of the work" (cxxx). "Reason" and "form" are abstractions from the apprehended, "felt" interrelations between distinguishable parts of a whole. Such interrelations I have made the central matter of my examination, attempting to resolve the theme to which the three "plots" are subservient.

Much Ado is not a "serious" play: it is "limited" in managing potentially serious matters with a deft nonchalance which passes by the possibility of some being sharp things that might cut. At the same time, it is a play full of themes which are to have sufficiently serious explorations and consequences in Shakespeare's later work. Othello's situation, for example, is a varient of Claudio's; just as Claudio's behaviour to Hero is a sketch of Bertram's (hurt pride turned spiteful: providing we do not

10 *Lectures on Shakespeare*, 1818.

11 *Timber, or Discoveries*, cxxviii.

see Claudio as only "mechanical"). Deceit by words (especially words of great meaning) is a constant in the tragi-comedies; and the comedy or farce of crediting too much of what is heard, or thought to be heard, is only the other side to "O love's best habit is in seeming trust," and the self-imposed deception by seeming and fair words which are found in the Sonnets.

Seeming and being in the later plays have a quite different serious-ness. But such a theme exists here, as it does in *1 Henry IV;* and if we say that the one is on *love* (and sex), the other on *honour,* then, looking ahead, the change in Shakespeare's playwriting is partially represented by *Much Ado* leading to *Measure for Measure;* and *1 Henry IV* leading to *Troilus and Cressida.* By this I suggest that potentially serious and distressing human situations (involving love and honour) are in *Much Ado* and *1 Henry IV* handled "lightly," as we say: contrived so as to keep them amusing, diverting, stimulating; but also so as to hold them more or less insulated from the deeper and more trenchant inquisitions into values of the tragi-comedies.

The place where we can hardly not notice little *points* of contact with the tragi-comedy outlook is the Church-scene. "Seeming" is harshly emphasized; Claudio seems on the edge of playing a part that would make it quite another *sort* of play; and the Friar's moral lines on lost affections — sad, uncomfortable thoughts — are echoed by the King in *All's Well.* But those points mark the real insulation of *Much Ado.* The disturbed feeling of *Measure for Measure* — its troubled thinking — is not here. We can hardly speak of "lack of feeling" in so bright, lively, glittering a piece: but is there not a certain *hard* quality, as with the bright colours of some Italian painting?

It is a *Decameron*-like story (barring the Watch), with some of the *Decameron* qualities of volatility in the persons, no wasting of sympathy on victims of jests, and the expectation of swift, unreflecting volte-faces of attitudes and emotions at the call of Fortune's pipe. That usually leaves an impression of shallowness, of a lack of *depth* of emotion, in northern European minds. The people seem rather heartless, while not in the least "cold"; and the stories are apt to leave us thinking more about "Now what did X really feel when . . . ?" than we know we *should.* In *Much Ado,* the brushing aside of the tone of calamity, the expecta-tions of volatile changes of feeling in Claudio, the jocular (for so it is) "Think not on him till to-morrow. I'll devise thee brave punishments for him. Strike up, pipers," only catch up a bright hardness (the result of a *deliberate* limitation of sympathies in the author?) which runs through the play.

Much Ado is a fantasy of equivocal appearances in a glittering world of amiable fools of all sorts. As naturally as Italians talk Italian, the

Messinans talk "equivocal"; but their "double tongues" are as harmless as those of the "spotted snakes" in *A Midsummer Night's Dream*. This equivocal quality, moreover, is deftly restricted to appearances: there are only the slightest touches of suggestion of any intrinsic equivocation in things themselves (in love, for example). Ambivalence is not a term to apply here.

These qualities urge me to "place" the play in the course of Shakespeare's writing as follows. In the breaking down of sensitive endurance, and of mental resistance to the revelation of the unfairness of human nature, there is a point where a sense of humour *fails;* where to see life and the world in humorous proportions is no longer possible: it cannot be assumed by an act of will, or, if so, the assumption cannot be maintained. At this point distresses distress, and cannot be accepted tolerantly as the world's way, muffled by an easy "they soon get over it" and by the cant of time. (I think of John Keats, of course; but without "Keatsifying" Shakespeare. In the *later* plays the "miseries of the world/ Are misery"; but not here in *Much Ado*). Immediately *before* that point, the besieged mind and invaded heart may defend themselves by the assumption of a certain hardness: assume the *Decameron virtu* — the trappings and the suits of *joy* — though they hath it not within. They may also find a certain high-flown gaiety — not hysterical, but making the best, and most, of the farce of human misunderstanding, deception, misprision — in the comedy of language (devised, so one may suppose, to communicate: but often used for just the reverse, either in game or in earnest). It is as if the sensitive mind and heart sought to persuade themselves by demonstration that life is a jest, and that the wider the comic net the likelier it is to resolve all the unmentioned but implied and subjective troubles in one great humorous or laughable plan, in which Fortune favours the laughers. This is the point at which great clowns who are melancholic — Chaplin, Raimu, Jouvet, Fernandel — stand and abide. One step from that strange equilibrium may turn to "cynicism" (especially in England): the cynicism where the attitudes I called "hardness" (self-defensive) and "farce" (offensive, debunking) combine to "place" love, honour, truth, only to devalue them. *Much Ado* stands in the Shakesperian canon just at that point.

GRAHAM STOREY

The Success of Much Ado about Nothing

MAY I confess that I only added the first words of my title when I was well into preparing this lecture? Do not mistake me: the riches of the play — the sheer exhilaration of the encounters between Benedick and Beatrice and their arabesques of wit; the superb stupidity of Dogberry and Verges and *their* arabesques of misunderstanding; the skilful weaving and disentanglement of the comic imbroglio — all these are a joy to see and hear, and belong to Shakespeare's most assured writing. But it is a commonplace of criticism that a successful play, like any other work of art, must be a unity: what Coleridge called the Imagination's "esemplastic power" must shape into one its individual forces and beauties. Whether *Much Ado* has this unity was the question that worried me.

It did not worry Shakespeare's contemporaries. The play offered an exciting Italianate melodrama, enlivened by two variegated sets of "humours": the wit-combats and properly-rewarded over-reachings of Benedick and Beatrice, and the low-life comedy of Dogberry and Verges; and remember that George Chapman and Ben Jonson had just started a run of fashionable "humour" plays. As in all proper comedies, the story came out all right in the end. "Strike up, pipers! *Dance.*" The formula ends that other comedy with a similarly riddling title, *As You Like It;* and whatever the differences of tone, the effect does not vary so much from that of the conclusion of *Twelfth Night,* the third of this group of plays written at the turn of the century:

> A great while ago the world begun,
> With hey, ho, the wind and the rain;
> But that's all one, our play is done,
> And we'll strive to please you every day.

The humours were what the contemporary audience remembered the

"The Success of 'Much Ado about Nothing'" by Graham Storey, from *More Talking of Shakespeare*, edited by John Garrett, © Longmans, Green & Co. Ltd. and Contributors 1959; reprinted with the permission of Theatre Arts Books, New York.

play by. "*Benedicte and Betteris*," say the Lord Treasurer's accounts for 1613: and *Much Ado* was almost certainly meant. "Benedick and Beatrice," wrote Charles I in his second Folio, as a second title to the play — exercising a similar Stuart prerogative in renaming *Twelfth Night* "The Tragedy of Malvolio." The "main plot" is clearly being regarded as a kind of serious relief to the much more absorbing comedy. When, with the Restoration, Shakespeare had to face the formidable canons of the neo-Classic critics, this central plot came in for some hard questioning. The criticism was, as we should expect, formal: the *decorum* was at fault. "The fable is absurd," writes Charles Gildon, in 1710, in an essay[1] often reprinted during the eighteenth century; "the charge against Hero is too shocking for tragedy or comedy, and Claudio's conduct is against the nature of love." He is almost equally concerned that the people of Messina do not act and talk, he says, like natives of a warm country.

But, at the turn of this century, one or two critics began to show a quite new uneasiness about the play. They found, not unity, not the almost unblemished gaiety that they found in *As You Like It* or *Twelfth Night;* but jarring tones, a gratuitous suffering and heartlessness in crisis — the Church Scene — that the rest of the play could not wipe out, and a distressing inconsistency in the characters of Claudio, the Prince and Leonato. The critical approaches were different: but the resultant *uncomfortableness* they generated was much the same. And it has undoubtedly left its mark upon many performances since.

The most frequent cause of uneasiness has been to respond to the play as though the protagonists were psychologically real. It is indeed the most expected response, as the dominant mode of the theatre is still naturalism. But it plays havoc with *Much Ado* as *comedy.* Stopford Brooke, writing in 1913[2] as a Bradleyan, shows what happens. He clearly wants to like the play; yet its very centre, the exposure in church, is, he writes, "a repulsive scene." "In it all the characters will be tried in the fire"; and, as a Victorian clergyman of strong, if sensitive views, he tries them. They emerge — Claudio, Don Pedro and Leonato — shallow, wilful, cruel, inconsistent with what they were before; and the play, its centre contaminated, is virtually handed over to Benedick and Beatrice. That, I am convinced, is not how Shakespeare wrote the play. But the figures of the main plot are bound to appear in this light, if we see them as fully-rounded characters and subject them to the tests of psychological consistency. I see them as something much nearer "masks": as not quite so far removed from the formalized figures of

[1] *Remarks on the Plays of Shakespeare:* included in *Shakespeare's Poems,* 1710 (supplementary vol. to Rowe's *Works of Shakespeare*).

[2] *Ten More Plays of Shakespeare,* 1913, p. 21.

Love's Labour's Lost, where most of the play's life resides in the plot-pattern and the dance of verbal wit, as many critics have suggested. I will return to this suggestion later. Meanwhile, I only want to insist that the opposite approach — that of naturalistic realism — stretches the play much further than a comedy can go, and makes almost impossible demands of the actors for the last two Acts. It can also lead to a quite ludicrous literalism, as where Stopford Brooke, quoting the magnificent absurd *finale* of Beatrice's outburst against Claudio after the Church Scene — "O God, that I were a man! I would eat his heart in the market-place" — solemnly comments, "Of course, she would not have done it."[3]

Others though, besides the "naturalist" critics, have found *Much Ado* disturbing: and disturbing because they do not discover in it the unity that I have made my main question. Sir Edmund Chambers,[4] writing fifty years ago, was probably the first to note what he called its "clashing of dramatic planes." "Elements," he wrote, "of tragedy, comedy, tragi-comedy, and farce are thrust together;" and the result is not unity, but "an unco-ordinated welter," a dramatic impressionism that sacrifices the whole to the brilliance of individual scenes or passages of dialogue or even individual lines. Other writers have more recently said much the same: the play's elements are incompatible; the plot too harsh for the characters; it is the wrong kind of romantic story to blend with comedy. "This happy play,"as "Q." called it in his Introduction to the *New Cambridge Shakespeare,* 1923, seems, in fact, to be in danger of losing its central place in the canon of Shakespeare's comedies (or it would be, if critics were taken too seriously).

I think that all these critics have seriously underrated the *comic* capacity of both Shakespeare and his audience: the capacity to create, and to respond to, varying and often contradictory experiences simultaneously; to create a pattern of human behaviour from their blendings and juxtapositions; and to obtain a keen enjoyment from seeing that pattern equally true at all levels. I will try to apply this claim to *Much Ado.* "For man is a giddy thing, and this is my conclusion," says Benedick in the last scene; and this is surely the play's "cause" or ruling theme. "Giddy," a favourite Elizabethan word: "light-headed, frivolous, flighty, inconstant," it meant by 1547; "whirling or circling round with bewildering rapidity" (1593); mentally intoxicated, "elated to thoughtlessness" (in Dr. Johnson's *Dictionary*). *Much Ado* has all these meanings in abundance. And Benedick's dictum, placed where it is, followed by

[3] Op. cit., p. 27: quoted by T. W. Craik in *Much Ado About Nothing* (*Scrutiny,* October 1953).

[4] Introduction to *Much Ado* (Red Letter Shakespeare, 1904–8). Reprinted in *Shakespeare: A Survey,* 1925.

the dance (reminiscent perhaps of the *La Ronde*-like Masked Ball of Act II), suggests eternal recurrence: "Man is a giddy thing" — and ever more will be so. The impetus to two of the play's three plots is the impetus to all the comedies, the propensity to love-making: one plot begins and ends with it; the other ends with it. And the impetus to the third plot, the antics of the Watch ("the vulgar humours of the play," said Gildon,[5] "are remarkably varied and distinguished"), is self-love: the innocent, thoughtless, outrageous love of Dogberry for himself and his position.

Inconstancy, mental intoxication, elation to thoughtlessness: the accompaniment of all these states is deception, self-deception, miscomprehension. And deception, the prelude to "giddiness," operates at every level of *Much Ado*. It is the common denominator of the three plots, and its mechanisms — eavesdroppings, mistakes of identity, disguises and maskings, exploited hearsay — are the major stuff of the play.

In the main plot — the Italian melodrama that Shakespeare took from Matteo Bandello, Bishop of Agen — the deception-theme is, of course, the most harshly obvious. Don John's instrument, Borachio, deceives "even the very eyes" of Claudio and the Prince; Claudio, the Prince and Leonato are all convinced that Hero has deceived them; Hero is violently deceived in her expectations of marriage, stunned by the slander; the Friar's plan to give her out as dead deceives everyone it is mean to.

The deceptions of Benedick and Beatrice in Leonato's garden-bower serve a function as a comic echo of all this. They are also beautifully-managed examples of a favourite Elizabethan device: the over-reacher over-reached, the "enginer hoist with his own petar," the marriage-mocker and husband-scorner taken in by — to us — a transparently obvious trick. (It is a major part of the play's delight that the audience always knows more than the actors: hints are dropped throughout; a Sophoclean comic irony pervades every incident.) Here, the metaphors of stalking and fishing are both deliberately overdone; and the effect is to emphasize that each of these eavesdroppings is a piece of play-acting, a mock-ceremonious game:

> DON PEDRO: Come hither, Leonato: what was it you told me of to-day, that your niece Beatrice was in love with Signior Benedick?
> CLAUDIO: O! ay: (Stalk on, stalk on; the fowl sits.) I did never think that lady would have loved any man.[6]

And in the next scene:

[5] Op. cit.
[6] II. iii. 98–103.

> URSULA: The pleasant'st angling is to see the fish
> Cut with her golden oars the silver stream,
> And greedily devour the treacherous bait:
> So angle we for Beatrice. . . .
> HERO: No, truly, Ursula, she is too disdainful;
> I know her spirits are as coy and wild
> As haggard of the rock.[7]

The contrast between prose and a delicate, artful blank verse makes sharper the difference of the fantasy each of them is offered. Benedick is given a superbly ludicrous caricature of a love-sick Beatrice, which only his own vanity could believe:

> CLAUDIO: Then down upon her knees she falls, weeps, sobs, beats her heart, tears her hair, prays, curses: "O sweet Benedick! God give me patience! . . ." Hero thinks surely she will die.[8]

And his own response, a mixture of comically solemn resolutions and illogical reasoning, is equally exaggerated:

> I must not seem proud: happy are they that hear their detractions, and can put them to mending. . . . No; the world must be peopled.[9]

Beatrice has her feminine vanity played on more delicately, but just as directly: she is given a not-too-exaggerated picture of herself as Lady Disdain, spiced with the praises of the man she is missing. And her response, in formal verse, clinches the success of the manoeuvre:

> What fire is in mine ears? Can this be true?
> Stand I condemn'd for pride and scorn so much?
> Contempt, farewell! and maiden pride, adieu!
> No glory lives behind the back of such. . . .[10]

"Elated to thoughtlessness" indeed (and particularly after all their earlier wit): but not only by a trick. Benedick and Beatrice are both, of course, perfect examples of self-deception: about their own natures, about the vanity their railing hides (and none the less vanity for its charm and wit), about the affection they are capable of—in need of— when the aggression is dropped, about their real relations to each other. This gives the theme of deception in their plot the higher, more

[7] III. i. 26 ff.
[8] II. iii. 162–5 and 191.
[9] Ibid., 248 ff.
[10] III. i. 107 ff.

permanent status of revelation. Hence much of its delight.

But no one in the play is more mentally intoxicated than Dogberry. He is king of all he surveys: of Verges, his perfect foil; of the Watch; of the peace of Messina at night. Only words — engines of deception — constantly trip him up; though, like Mrs. Malaprop, he sails on magnificently unaware:

> Dost thou not suspect my place? Dost thou not suspect my years? O that he were here to write me down an ass! . . . I am a wise fellow; and, which is more, an officer; and, which is more, a householder; and, which is more, as pretty a piece of flesh as any in Messina. . . .[11]

With Dogberry, the theme of giddiness, of self-deception, of revelling in the appearances that limitless vanity has made true for him, reaches miraculous proportions.

There is, though, the further meaning of "giddy," also, I suggested, warranted by Benedick's conclusion: "whirling or circling round." The structure of *Much Ado* — the melodramatic Italian love-story, enlivened by two humour-plots of Shakespeare's own invention — follows an established Elizabethan comedy-pattern: Chapman was to use it in *The Gentleman Usher* and *Monsieur d'Olive; Twelfth Night* — allowing for obvious differences in the tone of the central plot — is the obvious successor. Musically, we could call it a theme and variations. But you have merely to consider the Chapman comedies, where the two plots only arbitrarily meet — or Thomas Middleton, who brought in a collaborator to help him with the "echoing sub-plot" of his tragedy, *The Changeling* — to see Shakespeare's extraordinary structural skill here. "Faultless balance, blameless rectitude of design," said Swinburne: he is right, and it was not what most of his contemporaries recognized in *Much Ado*. But it still does not strongly enough suggest the grasp, the intellectual energy, that holds the play together and makes the kind of suggestions about reality in which the Elizabethan audience delighted. Here, again, Benedick's conclusion says more. Not only the play's wit — a microcosm of its total life — whirls and circles, with often deadly effect ("Thou hast frighted the word out of his right sense, so forcible is thy wit," cries Benedick to Beatrice in the last Act: it suggests that wit — and wit's author — can destroy or create at will) one of man's main instruments of living; but, in their vibrations and juxtapositions, the three plots do much the same.

Twice the plots fuse — once to advance the story, once to deepen it — and the achievement gives a peculiar exhilaration. Each time it is something of a shock; and then we see that, within the rules of probability

[11] IV. ii. 79 ff.

laid down by Aristotle for writers of tragedy (we can validly apply them to comedy too), it is wonderfully right that it should have happened like that.

The first occasion is the discovery by the Watch of the plot against Hero. When they line up to receive their instructions from Dogberry and Verges — on the principle of peace at all costs — it seems incredible that they should ever discover anything. But they do: though, admittedly, Shakespeare has to make Borachio drunk to make it possible. The Watch and their Officers are now locked firmly into the main plot, with all their ripples of absurdity; and the final dénouement is theirs. The innocent saved by the innocent, we may say; or, more likely (and certainly more Elizabethanly), the knaves caught out by the fools. "Is our whole dissembly appeared?" asks Dogberry, as he looks round for the rest of the Court. "Which be the malefactors?" asks the Sexton. "Marry, that am I and my partner," answers Dogberry, with pride.

However we look at it, the impact has clearly changed the status of the villains. "Ducdame, ducdame, ducdame," sings Jaques (it is his own verse) to his banished companions in the Forest of Arden. "What's that 'ducdame'?" asks Amiens. " 'Tis a Greek invocation to call fools into a circle." Here in *Much Ado*, the knaves have been thrust in with the fools: if it makes the fools feel much more important than they are, it makes the villains much less villainous; or villainous in a way that disturbs us less. This is one device by which the interlocking of plots establishes the play's unity, and, in doing so, creates a new, more inclusive tone.

The entry of the Watch into the centre of the play advances the story. The entry of Benedick and Beatrice, in that short packed dialogue after the Church Scene, where they declare their belief in Hero and their love for each other, seems as though it must do so too; but in fact it does not. Rather, it does not if we see the heart of the play now as Hero's vindication. That is brought about without help from Benedick; and, indeed, Benedick's challenge to Claudio, vehemently undertaken and dramatically presented, is, by the end of the play, treated very casually: only perfunctorily recalled, and easily brushed aside in the general mirth and reconciliation of the ending. Perhaps, then, this scene *removes* the play's centre, puts it squarely in the Benedick and Beatrice plot? That is how many critics have taken it; and what, for example, was in "Q."'s' mind when he wrote of the scene's climax: " 'Kill Claudio!' These two words nail the play"; and again, ". . . at this point undoubtedly Shakespeare transfers [the play] from *novella* to drama — to a real spiritual conflict."[12] It is certainly how many

12 Op. cit., pp. xiii and xv.

producers and actors — with understandable temptation — have interpreted the scene.

Much Ado demands, of course, a continual switching of interest. We
focus it in turn on Benedick and Beatrice, on Hero and Claudio, on
Don John and Borachio, on Dogberry and Verges, back to Hero and
Claudio, and so on. This gives something of the controlled whirl and
circling motion I have commented on. It is also true that this scene
between Benedick and Beatrice has a new seriousness; that their shared,
intuitive belief in Hero's innocence has deepened their relations with
each other, and our attitude towards them. But that is not the same
as saying that the play has become something different, or that its
centre has shifted. That would seriously jeopardize its design; and,
although there *are* flaws in the play, I am sure that its design is what
Shakespeare intended it to be.

The play's true centre is in fact neither a plot nor a group of characters, but a theme: Benedick's conclusion about man's giddiness, his
irresistible propensity to be taken in by appearances. It is a theme that
must embody an *attitude;* and it is the attitude here that provides *Much
Ado*'s complexity: its disturbingness (where it does disturb); its ambiguities, where the expected response seems far from certain; but its inclusiveness too, where it is assured. For Shakespeare's approach to this
theme at the turn of the century (one could call it the major theme of his
whole writing-life, probed at endlessly varying levels) was far from
simple. The riddling titles of the group of comedies written within these
two years, 1598–1600, are deceptive, or at any rate ambiguous. *Much
Ado About Nothing, As You Like It, Twelfth Night; or, What You Will:*
these can all, as titles, be interpreted lightly, all but cynically, as leaving
it to the audience how to take them with a disarming, amused casualness.
Or, equally, they can leave room for manoeuvre, include several attitudes, without committing themselves to any. This blending or jostling
of sympathies is sufficiently evident in these comedies to have won for
itself the status of a convention. Dr. M. C. Bradbrook, who has lov-
ingly pursued all the conventions of the Elizabethan theatre, has called
it "polyphonic music";[13] Mr. S. L. Bethell, more directly concerned
with the Elizabethan audience, calls their capacity to respond to difficult
aspects of the same situation, simultaneously, but in often contradictory ways, "multi-consciousness."[14] *Much Ado* exhibits the one and
demands the other in the highest degree.

We must, I think, respond in much the same way as the Elizabethan
audience did, if we are to appreciate to the full the scene between

---

[13] In *Shakespeare and Elizabethan Poetry*, 1951: the title of Chapter X.
[14] In *Shakespeare and the Popular Dramatic Tradition*, 1948, *passim.*

Benedick and Beatrice in the church; and that oddly-tempered, but still powerful scene of Leonato's outbursts to Antonio at the beginning of Act V. For both these scenes, however different — the first is set in a half-comic key, the second employs a rhetoric that is nearer the formally "tragic" — employ deliberate ambiguities of tone and demand a double response.

I will examine the Benedick and Beatrice scene first. Here, Shakespeare clearly means us to sympathize with Beatrice's vehement attacks on Claudio on Hero's behalf, and with the mounting strength of Benedick's allegiance to her. At the same time, he overdoes the vehemence, exposes it to the comedy of his wry appraisal, brings both characters to the edge of delicate caricature. The scene's climax (I have quoted "Q." 's remarks on it) has been taken to show the maximum deployment of Shakespeare's sympathy. It also exhibits perfectly his comedy. Benedick and Beatrice have just protested they love each other with all their heart:

> BENEDICK: Come, bid me do anything for thee.
> BEATRICE: Kill Claudio.
> BENEDICK: Ha! not for the wide world.
> BEATRICE: You kill me to deny it. Farewell.[15]

Superbly dramatic: three fresh shocks in three lines; and, with each, a new insight into human nature; but also highly ironical. To demand the killing of Claudio, in the world established by the play, is ridiculous. To refuse it at once, after the avowal to do *anything*, equally so, however right Benedick may be ethically (and the irony demands that he refuse *at once*: I am sure Dr. Bradbrook[16] is wrong in saying that he hesitates). And for Beatrice, upon this refusal, to take back her heart, having given it a moment before, completes the picture: passionately generous to her wronged cousin, if we isolate the exchange and treat it as a piece of magnificent impressionism; heroic, absurd and a victim to passion's deception, if we see it — as we surely must — within the context of the whole play.

Mr. T. W. Craik, in an admirably close analysis of *Much Ado* in *Scrutiny*,[17] makes this scene between Benedick and Beatrice a pivot of the play's values. It is, he says, " 'placed' by the scene's beginning [i.e. the earlier events in the church]. Putting the point crudely, it represents the triumph of emotion over reason; the reasonableness of Friar

---

[15] IV. i. 293–296.
[16] Op. cit., p. 183.
[17] October 1953, op. cit.

Francis's plan for Claudio and Hero. . . ."[18] I agree with him when he goes on to say that "emotion's triumph" is laughable in Benedick (though I think he exaggerates its extent). But surely it is an over-simplification to identify Shakespeare's attitude — as he seems to do more explicitly later in his essay[19] — with the Friar's common sense. The Friar is essential to the plot (and much more competent in guiding it than his brother of *Romeo and Juliet*); and his calm sanity admirably "places" Leonato's hysteria in the Church Scene. But the whole spirit of the play seems to me antagonistic to any *one* attitude's dominating it. And the second scene I want to examine — Leonato and Antonio in v. i. — appears to bear this out.

For here Antonio begins as the repository of the Friar's wisdom, as the Stoic, calming Leonato down. Yet, as experience floods in on him — the memory of wrong in the shape of Don Pedro and Claudio — he too becomes "flesh and blood," and ends up by out-doing Leonato:

> What, man! I know them, yea,
> And what they weigh, even to the utmost scruple,
> Scrambling, out-facing, fashion-monging boys,
> That lie and cog and flout, deprave and slander,
> Go antickly, show outward hideousness,
> And speak off half a dozen dangerous words,
> How they might hurt their enemies, if they durst;
> And this is all!
> LEONATO: But, brother Antony,[20]

The roles are neatly reversed. But the invective is too exuberantly Shakespearian to be merely — or even mainly — caricature. Can we say the same of Leonato's outburst that begins the scene?

> I pray thee, cease thy counsel,
> which falls into mine ears as profitless
> As water in a sieve: Give not me counsel; . . .[21]

Considered realistically, it must make us uneasy. Leonato knows (Antonio does not) that Hero is in fact alive: to that extent, most of his emotion is counterfeit. Again, we remember his hysterical self-pity of the Act before, when his attitude to his daughter was very different:

> Do not live, Hero; do not ope thine eyes;
> . . . Griev'd I, I had but one?

[18] p. 308.
[19] p. 314.
[20] v. i. 92–9.
[21] v. i. 3–5.

> Chid I for that at frugal nature's frame?
> O! one too much by thee. Why had I one?
> Why ever wast thou lovely in mine eyes?[22]

To some extent, he is still dramatizing himself in this scene, still enjoying his grief. But his language is no longer grotesque or self-convicting, as that was. He echoes a theme — "experience against auctoritee," the Middle Ages called it — which in *Romeo and Juliet* had been nearer a set piece:

> FRIAR LAURENCE: Let me dispute with thee of thy estate.
> ROMEO: Thou canst not speak of that thou dost not feel. . . .[23]

but here it has a new authenticity in movement and image:

> for, brother, men
> Can counsel and speak comfort to that grief
> Which they themselves not feel; but, tasting it,
> Their counsel turns to passion, which before
> Would give preceptial medicine to rage,
> Fetter strong madness in a silken thread,
> Charm ache with air and agony with words.[24]

Again, as with Benedick and Beatrice, the whole scene, ending with the challenge of Claudio and the Prince to a duel, presents a mixture of tones: appeal to our sympathy, exaggeration which is on or over the edge of comedy.

Both these scenes, peripheral to the main plot, but of the essence of the play's art, demand, if they are to be fully appreciated, a complex response. What, then, of the crux of *Much Ado,* the shaming of Hero in church? On any realistic view it must, as has been said, be a repulsive scene: an innocent girl slandered and shamed by her betrothed, with apparently deliberate calculation, during her marriage-service, and in front of her father — the city's Governor — and the whole congregation. However we see it, Shakespeare's writing here is sufficiently powerful to give us some wincing moments. No interpretation can take away the shock of Claudio's brutal

> There, Leonato, take her back again:
> Give not this rotten orange to your friend;[25]

[22] IV. i. 125, 129–32.
[23] III. iii. 62–3.
[24] V. i. 20–6.
[25] IV. i. 31–2.

or of the Prince's heartless echo:

> What should I speak?
> I stand dishonour'd, that have gone about
> To link my dear friend to a common stale.

The clipped exchange between Leonato and Don John that follows seems to give the lie the ring of finality, to make false true in front of our eyes:

> LEONATO: Are these things spoken, or do I but dream?
> DON JOHN: Sir, they are spoken, and these things are true.

The generalizing assent, helped by the closed-circle form of question and answer, has a claustrophobic effect on both Hero and us (I think of the nightmare world of "double-think" closing in in Orwell's *Nineteen Eighty-Four*: this is a verbal nightmare too). Momentarily, we have left Messina and might well be in the meaner, darker world of that later play of similarly quibbling title, but much less pleasant implications, *All's Well That Ends Well*. There "these things" are commented on by a Second French Lord, who knows human nature; knows Parolles and his hollowness: "Is it possible he should know what he is, and be that he is?"; and Bertram and his meanness: "As we are ourselves, what things are we!" ("Merely our own traitors," adds the First Lord, almost redundantly.)

Then, with a jolt, we remember that "these things" are *not* true. They are not true *in* the play, which is the first thing to remind ourselves of, if we wish to preserve the play's balance as comedy. For in the later and so-called "Problem Comedies" (tragi-comedies, I prefer to follow A. P. Rossiter in calling them) — *All's Well, Troilus and Cressida, Measure for Measure* — such accusations *are* true, or would be true if those accused of them had had their way — had not been tricked into doing something quite different from what they thought they were doing (Cressida comes into the first category; Bertram and Angelo into the second). But here the characters are playing out an act of deception, each of them (except Don John) unaware in fact of what the truth is. To that extent, they are all innocent, Claudio and the Prince as well as Hero: played on by the plot, not (as we sense wherever tragic feeling enters) playing it, willing it. The *situation* is in control.

Secondly, they are not true *outside* the play. To state that at all probably sounds absurd. But genuine tragic feeling in Shakespeare forces its extra-theatrical truth on us: continuously in the tragedies, spasmodically — but still disturbingly — in the tragi-comedies. We know only too well how permanently true are *Hamlet, Othello, Macbeth*. But the exposures of the tragi-comedies (Hero's shaming by no means exhausts the *genre*) inflict on us truths about human nature — we may prefer to call them half-truths. "But man, proud man," cries out Isabella (and she has every justification),

> Drest in a little brief authority,
> Most ignorant of what he's most assur'd,
> His glassy essence, like an angry ape,
> Plays such fantastic tricks before high heaven
> As make the angels weep; who, with our spleens,
> Would all themselves laugh mortal.[26]

Here, all the possibilities of human nature are on the stage. We are *involved with* the people who are hurt or betrayed or even exposed (Angelo, as he cries out on the "blood" that has betrayed him, is potentially a tragic figure); we are involved too in the language and its searing comments on human frailty or baseness.

But go back to the scene in *Much Ado*, and, after the first shock, we are no longer fully involved. First, because the identities of Hero and Claudio have been kept to an irreducible minimum. That is why I earlier called them "masks." They have a part to play in a situation that is the climax to the whole play's theme; but they have not the core of being — or of dramatic being — which suffers or deliberately causes suffering. It would be quite different — ghastly and impossible — to imagine Beatrice in Hero's position.

And, secondly, the whole scene's deliberate *theatricality* lessens our involvement and distances our emotions. It emphasizes that it is, after all, only a play and intended for our entertainment;[27] we know that the accusation of Hero is false and — as this is a comedy — is bound to be put right by the end. First Claudio, then Leonato, takes the centre of the stage: the effect is to diminish any exclusively tragic concern for Hero, as we appraise the responses of the other two. There can be no doubt about Leonato's: it is highly exaggerated and hovers on the edge of caricature. We recognize the tones from *Romeo and Juliet*. There, vindictive, absurd old Capulet hustles Juliet on to a marriage she abhors; and then, in a stylized, cruelly comic scene, is shown (with his wife and the Nurse) over-lamenting her when she feigns death to avoid it. Shakespeare has little pity for this kind of selfishness. Here, as Leonato inveighs against his daughter — now in a swoon — we have self-pity

---

26 *Measure for Measure*, II. ii. 117–23.

27 S. L. Bethell makes the same point about the ill-treatment of Malvolio: op. cit., pp. 33–4.

masking itself as righteous indignation: the repetitions show where his real interest lies:

> But mine, and mine I lov'd, and mine I prais'd,
> And mine that I was proud on, mine so much
> That I myself was to myself not mine,
> Valuing of her . . . [28]

Yet, as he goes on, the tone alters, as so often in this volatile, quick-changing play:

> . . . why, she — O! she is fallen
> Into a pit of ink, that the wide sea
> Hath drops too few to wash her clean again,
> And salt too little which may season give
> To her foul tainted flesh.[29]

That is still over-violent, but the images of Hero's stain and of the sea failing to make her clean introduce a different note. We have heard it in Claudio's accusation:

> Behold! how like a maid she blushes here.
> O! what authority and show of truth
> Can cunning sin cover itself withal. . . .[30]

and in his outburst against seeming: "Out on thee! Seeming! I will write against it. . . ."

Again, there is more here than his earlier, calculated stage-management of the scene. It is as though the situation has suddenly taken charge, become horribly true for a moment; and as if Shakespeare has injected into it some of the disgust at sexual betrayal we know from the dark Sonnets and from the crises of a host of later plays: *Measure for Measure, Troilus and Cressida, Hamlet, Othello, Cymbeline.*

This apparent intrusion of something alien — seemingly personal — into the very centre of the play was what had led me to doubt its success. I was wrong, I think (and it follows that I think other doubters are wrong), for three reasons. First, the intrusion, the cold music, is only a touch; one of several themes that make up the scene. Its language is harsh, but chimes in with nothing else in the play: no deadly vibrations or echoes are set up. Compare Claudio and Leonato with Troilus or Isabella, or, even more, with Hamlet or Othello, in whose words we

[28] iv. i. 138–41.
[29] Ibid., 141–5.
[30] iv. i. 34–6.

feel a wrenching, an almost physical dislocation of set attitudes and beliefs: and the outbursts here have something of the isolated, artificial effect of set speeches.

Secondly, the play's central theme — of deception, miscomprehension, man's "giddiness" at every level — is dominant enough to claim much of our response in *every* scene: including this climax in the church that embodies it most harshly, but most fully. And, in its many-sidedness and "many-tonedness," this theme is, as I have tried to show, one well within the tradition of Elizabethan comedy.

Thirdly, and lastly, the *tone* of *Much Ado* — animated, brittle, observant, delighting in the ado men make — does not have to stretch itself much to accommodate the moments of questioning in the church. And this tone is ultimately, I think, what we most remember of the play: what gives it its genuine difference from *As You Like It* and *Twelfth Night*. Although two of its most loved figures are Warwickshire yokels (and nothing could change them), the aura of Bandello's Italian plot pervades the rest. The love of sharp wit and the love of melodrama belong there; so do the sophisticated, unsentimental tone, and the ubiquitous, passed-off classical references: to Cupid and Hercules, Leander and Troilus. Gildon was wrong: in essentials, the people of Messina *do* act and talk like natives of a warm country.

The tone I mean is most apparent — most exhilarating and most exacting — in the wit-flytings between Benedick and Beatrice; but it dominates the word-play throughout: and this is one of the most word-conscious and wittiest of all Shakespeare's comedies. If I have said little about the words and the wit, this is because no one was more at home there, and could better communicate his enjoyment of them, than the late A. P. Rossiter: and you can read his lecture[31] on the play from one of the last of his memorable Shakespeare courses at Cambridge. My own debt to him will be very clear to all of you who heard his many lectures here at Stratford.

---

31 One of twelve lectures given at Stratford and Cambridge, published in 1959 by Longmans.

HELEN GARDNER

As You Like It

As its title declares, this is a play to please all tastes. It is the last play in the world to be solemn over, and there is more than a touch of absurdity in delivering a lecture, particularly on a lovely summer morning, on this radiant blend of fantasy, romance, wit and humor. The play itself provides its own ironic comment on anyone who attempts to speak about it: "You have said; but whether wisely or no, let the forest judge."

For the simple, it provides the stock ingredients of romance: a handsome, well-mannered young hero, the youngest of three brothers, two disguised princesses to be wooed and wed, and a banished, virtuous Duke to be restored to his rightful throne. For the more sophisticated, it propounds, in the manner of the old courtly literary form of the *débat*, a question which is left to us to answer: Is it better to live in the court or the country? "How like you this shepherd's life, Master Touchstone?," asks Corin, and receives a fool's answer: "Truly, shepherd, in respect of itself, it is a good life; but in respect that it is a shepherd's life, it is naught. In respect that it is solitary, I like it very well; but in respect that it is private, it is a very vile life." Whose society would you prefer, Le Beau's or Audrey's? Would you rather be gossiped at in the court or gawped at in the country? The play has also the age-old appeal of the pastoral, and in different forms. The pastoral romance of princesses playing at being a shepherd boy and his sister is combined with the pastoral love-eclogue in the wooing of Phoebe, with the burlesque of this in the wooing of Audrey, and with the tradition of the moral eclogue, in which the shepherd is the wise man, in Corin. For the learned and literary this is one of Shakespeare's most allusive plays, uniting old traditions and playing with them lightly. Then there are the songs — the forest is full of music — and there is spectacle: a wrestling match to delight lovers of sport, the procession with the deer, which goes

"As You Like It" by Helen Gardner, from *More Talking About Shakespeare*, edited by John Garrett, © Longmans, Green & Co. Ltd. and Contributors 1959; reprinted with the permission of Theatre Arts Books, New York.

back to old country rituals and folk plays, and finally the masque of
Hymen, to end the whole with courtly grace and dignity. This is an
image of civility and true society, for Hymen is a god of cities, as
Milton knew:

> There let *Hymen* oft appear
> In Saffron robe, with Taper clear,
> And pomp, and feast, and revelry,
> With mask, and antique Pageantry.

The only thing the play may be said to lack, when compared with Shakespeare's other comedies, is broad humor, the humor of gross clowns.
William makes only a brief appearance. The absence of clowning may
be due to an historic reason, the loss of Kempe, the company's funny
man. But if this was the original reason for the absence of pure clowning, Shakespeare has turned necessity to glorious gain and made a play
in which cruder humors would be out of place. *As You Like It* is the
most refined and exquisite of the comedies, the one which is most con-
sistently played over by a delighted intelligence. It is Shakespeare's
most Mozartian comedy.

The basic story is a folk tale. The ultimate sources for the plots of
Shakespeare's greatest tragedy and his most unflawed comedy are stories
of the same kind. The tale of the old king who had three daughters, of
whom the elder two were wicked and the youngest was good, belongs
to the same primitive world of the imagination as the tale of the knight
who had three sons, the eldest of whom was wicked and robbed the
youngest, who was gallant and good, of his inheritance. The youngest
son triumphed, like Jack the Giant Killer, over a strong man, a wrestler,
joined a band of outlaws in the forest, became their king, and with the
aid of an old servant of his father, the wily Adam Spencer, in the end
had his revenge on his brother and got his rights. Lodge retained some
traces of the boisterous elements of this old story; but Shakespeare
omitted them. His Orlando is no bully, threatening and blustering and
breaking down the doors to feast with his boon companions in his brother's house. He is brave enough and quick-tempered; but he is above all
gentle. On this simple story Lodge grafted a pastoral romance in his
Rosalynde. He made the leader of the outlaws a banished Duke, and
gave both exiled Duke and tyrant usurper only daughters, as fast friends
as their fathers are sworn enemies. The wrestling match takes place at
the tyrant's court and is followed by the banishment of Rosalynde and
the flight of the two girls to the forest, disguised as shepherd and
shepherdess. There the shepherd boy is wooed by the gallant hero, and
arouses a passion of lovesickness in a shepherdess who scorns her faithful

lover. The repentance of the wicked brother and his flight to the forest provide the necessary partner for the tyrant's good daughter, and all ends happily with marriages and the restoration of the good Duke. Shakespeare added virtually nothing to the plot of Lodge's novel. There is no comedy in which, in one sense, he invents so little. He made the two Dukes into brothers. Just as in *King Lear* he put together two stories of good and unkind children, so here he gives us two examples of a brother's unkindness. This adds to the fairy-tale flavor of the plot, because it turns the usurping Duke into a wicked uncle. But if he invents no incidents, he leaves out a good deal. Besides omitting the blusterings of Rosader (Orlando), he leaves out a final battle and the death in battle of the usurping Duke, preferring to have him converted offstage by a chance meeting with a convenient and persuasive hermit. In the same way he handles very cursorily the repentance of the wicked brother and his good fortune in love. In Lodge's story, the villain is cast into prison by the tyrant who covets his estates. In prison he repents, and it is as a penitent that he arrives in the forest. Shakespeare also omits the incident of the attack on Ganymede and Aliena by robbers, in which Rosader is overpowered and wounded and Saladyne (Oliver) comes to the rescue and drives off the assailants. As has often been pointed out, this is both a proof of the genuineness of his repentance and a reason, which many critics of the play have felt the want of, for Celia's falling in love. Maidens naturally fall in love with brave young men who rescue them. But Shakespeare needs to find no "reasons for loving" in this play in which a dead shepherd's saw is quoted as a word of truth: "Whoever lov'd that lov'd not at first sight." He has far too much other business in hand at the center and heart of his play to find time for mere exciting incidents. He stripped Lodge's plot down to the bare bones, using it as a kind of frame, and created no subplot of his own. But he added four characters. Jaques, the philosopher, bears the same name as the middle son of Sir Rowland de Boys — the one whom Oliver kept at his books — who does not appear in the play until he turns up casually at the end as a messenger. It seems possible that the melancholy Jaques began as this middle son and that his melancholy was in origin a scholar's melancholy. If so, the character changed as it developed, and by the time that Shakespeare had fully conceived his cynical spectator he must have realized that he could not be kin to Oliver and Orlando. The born solitary must have no family: Jaques seems the quintessential only child. To balance Jaques, as another kind of commentator, we are given Touchstone, critic and parodist of love and lovers and of court and courtiers. And, to make up the full consort of pairs to be mated, Shakespeare invented two rustic lovers, William and Audrey, dumb yokel and sluttish goat-girl. These additional characters add nothing at all to the story. If you were to tell it you would leave them out. They show us that story was not Shakespeare's concern in this play; its soul is not to be looked for there. If you were to go to *As You Like It* for the story you would, in Johnson's phrase, "hang yourself."

In an essay called "The Basis of Shakespearian Comedy"[1] Professor Nevill Coghill attempted to "establish certain things concerning the nature of comic form, as it was understood at Shakespeare's time." He pointed out that there were two conceptions of comedy current in the sixteenth century, both going back to grammarians of the fourth century, but radically opposed to each other. By the one definition a comedy was a story beginning in sadness and ending in happiness. By the other it was, in Sidney's words, "an imitation of the common errors of our life" represented "in the most ridiculous and scornefull sort that may be; so that it is impossible that any beholder can be content to be such a one." Shakespeare, he declared, accepted the first; Jonson, the second. But although *As You Like It*, like *A Midsummer Night's Dream*, certainly begins in sadness and ends with happiness, I do not feel, when we have said this, that we have gone very far toward defining the play's nature, and I do not think that the plot in either of these two lovely plays, or in the enchanting early comedy *Love's Labor's Lost*, which indeed has hardly any plot at all, can be regarded as the "soul" or animating force of Shakespeare's most original and characteristic comedies. Professor Coghill's formula fits plays which we feel rather uneasy about, *The Merchant of Venice* and *Measure for Measure*. It is precisely the stress on the plot which makes us think of these as being more properly described as tragi-comedies than comedies. Neither of them is a play which we would choose as a norm of Shakespeare's genius in comedy. In *As You Like It* the plot is handled in the most perfunctory way. Shakespeare crams his first act with incident in order to get everyone to the forest as soon as he possibly can and, when he is ready, he ends it all as quickly as possible. A few lines dispose of Duke Frederick, and leave the road back to his throne empty for Duke Senior. As for the other victim of a wicked brother, it is far more important that Orlando should marry Rosalind than that he should be restored to his rights.

Mrs. Suzanne Langer, in her brilliant and suggestive book *Feeling and Form*,[2] has called comedy an image of life triumphing over chance. She declares that the essence of comedy is that it embodies in symbolic form our sense of happiness in feeling that we can meet and master the changes and chances of life as it confronts us. This seems to me to provide a good description of what we mean by "pure comedy," as

[1] *Essays and Studies* (English Association: John Murray, 1950).
[2] Routledge, 1953.

distinct from the corrective or satirical comedy of Jonson. The great symbol of pure comedy is marriage by which the world is renewed, and its endings are always instinct with a sense of fresh beginnings. Its rhythm is the rhythm of the life of mankind, which goes on and renews itself as the life of nature does. The rhythm of tragedy, on the other hand, is the rhythm of the individual life which comes to a close, and its great symbol is death. The one inescapable fact about every human being is that he must die. No skill in living, no sense of life, no inborn grace or acquired wisdom can avert this individual doom. A tragedy, which is played out under the shadow of an inevitable end, is an image of the life pattern of every one of us. A comedy, which contrives an end which is not implicit in its beginning, and which is, in itself, a fresh beginning, is an image of the flow of human life. The young wed, so that they may become in turn the older generation, whose children will wed, and so on, as long as the world lasts. Comedy pictures what Rosalind calls "the full stream of the world." At the close of a tragedy we look back over a course which has been run: "the rest is silence." The end of a comedy declares that life goes on: "Here we are all over again." Tragic plots must have a logic which leads to an inescapable conclusion. Comic plots are made up of changes, chances and surprises. Coincidences can destroy tragic feeling: they heighten comic feeling. It is absurd to complain in poetic comedy of improbable encounters and characters arriving pat on their cue, of sudden changes of mind and mood by which an enemy becomes a friend. Puck, who creates and presides over the central comedy of *A Midsummer Night's Dream,* speaks for all comic writers and lovers of true comedy when he says:

> And those things do best please me
> That befall preposterously.

This aspect of life, as continually changing and presenting fresh opportunities for happiness and laughter, poetic comedy idealizes and presents to us by means of fantasy. Fantasy is the natural instrument of comedy, in which plot, which is the "soul" of tragedy, is of secondary importance, an excuse for something else. After viewing a tragedy we have an "acquist of true experience" from a "great event." There are no "events" in comedy; there are only "happenings." Events are irreversible and comedy is not concerned with the irreversible, which is why it must always shun the presentation of death. In adapting Lodge's story Shakespeare did not allow Charles the wrestler to kill the Franklin's sons. Although they are expected to die, we may hope they will recover from their broken ribs. And he rejected also Lodge's ending in which the wicked Duke was killed in battle, preferring his improbable conversion by a hermit. But why should we complain of its improbability? It is only in tragedy that second chances are not given. Comedy is full of purposes mistook, not "falling on the inventor's head" but luckily misfiring altogether. In comedy, as often happens in life, people are mercifully saved from being as wicked as they meant to be.

Generalization about the essential distinctions between tragedy and comedy is called in question, when we turn to Shakespeare, by the inclusiveness of his vision of life. In the great majority of his plays the elements are mixed. But just as he wrote one masterpiece which is purely tragic, dominated by the conception of Fate, in *Macbeth*, so he wrote some plays which embody a purely comic vision. Within the general formula that "a comedy is a play with a happy ending," which can, of course, include tragicomedies, he wrote some plays in which the story is a mere frame and the essence of the play lies in the presentation of an image of human life, not as an arena for heroic endeavor but as a place of encounters.

Tragedy is presided over by time, which urges the hero onward to fulfill his destiny. In Shakespeare's comedies time goes by fits and starts. It is not so much a movement onward as a space in which to work things out: a midsummer night, a space too short for us to feel time's movement, or the unmeasured time of *As You Like It* or *Twelfth Night*. The comedies are dominated by a sense of place rather than of time. In Shakespeare's earliest comedy it is not a very romantic place: the city of Ephesus. Still, it is a place where two pairs of twins are accidentally reunited, and their old father, in danger of death at the beginning, is united to his long-lost wife at the close. The substance of the play is the comic plot of mistakings, played out in a single place on a single day. The tragicomic story of original loss and final restoration provides a frame. In what is probably his second comedy, *The Two Gentlemen of Verona*, Shakespeare tried a quite different method. The play is a dramatization of a *novella*, and it contains no comic place of encounters where time seems to stand still. The story begins in Verona, passes to Milan, and ends in a forest between the two cities. None of these places exerts any hold upon our imaginations. The story simply moves forward through them. In *Love's Labor's Lost*, by contrast, Shakespeare went as far as possible in the other direction. The whole play is a kind of ballet of lovers and fantastics, danced out in the King of Navarre's park. Nearby is a village where Holofernes is the schoolmaster, Nathaniel the curate, and Dull the constable. In this play we are given, as a foil to the lords and ladies, not comic servants, parasitic on their masters, but a little comic world, society in miniature, going about its daily business while the lovers are engaged in the discovery of theirs. Shakespeare dispensed with the tragicomic frame altogether here. There is no sorrow at the beginning, only youthful male fatuity; and the "putting right" at the close lies in the chastening of the lords by the ladies. The picture of the course of life as it appears to the comic vision, with young men falling in love and young women testing their suitors, and other men "laboring in their vocations" to keep the world turning and to impress their fellows, is the whole matter of the play. Much more magical than the sunlit park of the King of Navarre is the wood near Athens where Puck plays the part of chance. Shakespeare reverted here to the structural pattern of his earliest comedy, beginning with the cruel fury of Egeus against his daughter, the rivalry of Lysander and Demetrius and the unhappiness of the scorned Helena, and ending with Theseus's overriding of the father's will and the proper pairing of the four lovers. But here he not only set his comic plot of mistakings within a frame of sorrow turning to joy, he also set his comic place of encounters apart from the real world, the palace where the play begins and ends. All the center of the play takes place in the moonlit wood where lovers immortal and mortal quarrel, change partners, are blinded, and have their eyes purged.

Having created a masterpiece, Shakespeare, who never repeated a success, went back in his next play to tragicomedy, allowing the threat of terrible disaster to grow through the play up to a great dramatic fourth act. *The Merchant of Venice* has what *The Two Gentlemen of Verona* lacks, an enchanted place. Belmont, where Bassanio goes to find his bride, and where Lorenzo flees with Jessica, and from which Portia descends like a goddess to solve the troubles of Venice, is a place apart, "above the smoke and stir." But it is not, like the wood near Athens, a place where the changes and chances of our mortal life are seen mirrored. It stands too sharply over against Venice, a place of refuge rather than a place of discovery. *Much Ado About Nothing* reverts to the single place of *The Comedy of Errors* and *Love's Labor's Lost;* and its tragicomic plot, which also comes to a climax in a dramatic scene in the fourth act, is lightened not by a shift of scene but by its interweaving with a brilliant comic plot, and by all kinds of indications that all will soon be well again. The trouble comes in the middle of this play: at the beginning, as at the end, all is revelry and happiness. A sense of holiday, of time off from the world's business, reigns in Messina. The wars are over, peace has broken out, and Don Pedro and the gentlemen have returned to where the ladies are waiting for them to take up again the game of love and wit. In the atmosphere created by the first act Don John's malice is a cloud no bigger than a man's hand. And although it grows as the play proceeds, the crisis of the fourth act is like a heavy summer thundershower which darkens the sky for a time but will, we know, soon pass. The brilliant lively city of

Messina is a true place of mistakings and discoveries, like the park of the King of Navarre; but, also like the park of the King of Navarre, it lacks enchantment. It is too near the ordinary world to seem more than a partial image of human life. In *As You Like It* Shakespeare returned to the pattern of *A Midsummer Night's Dream*, beginning his play in sorrow and ending it with joy, and making his place of comic encounters a place set apart from the ordinary world.

The Forest of Arden ranks with the wood near Athens and Prospero's island as a place set apart, even though, unlike them, it is not ruled by magic. It is set over against the envious court ruled by a tyrant, and a home which is no home because it harbors hatred, not love. Seen from the court it appears untouched by the discontents of life, a place where "they fleet the time carelessly, as they did in the golden age," the gay greenwood of Robin Hood. But, of course, it is no such Elysium. It contains some unamiable characters. Corin's master is churlish and Sir Oliver Martext is hardly sweet-natured; William is a dolt and Audrey graceless. Its weather, too, is by no means always sunny. It has a bitter winter. To Orlando, famished with hunger and supporting the fainting Adam, it is "an uncouth forest" and a desert where the air is bleak. He is astonished to find civility among men who

> in this desert inaccessible,
> Under the shade of melancholy boughs,
> Lose and neglect the creeping hours of time.

In fact Arden does not seem very attractive at first sight to the weary escapers from the tyranny of the world. Rosalind's "Well, this is the forest of Arden" does not suggest any very great enthusiasm; and to Touchstone's "Ay, now I am in Arden; the more fool I: when I was at home, I was in a better place: but travelers must be content," she can only reply "Ay, be so, good Touchstone." It is as if they all have to wake up after a good night's rest to find what a pleasant place they have come to. Arden is not a place for the young only. Silvius, forever young and forever loving, is balanced by Corin, the old shepherd, who reminds us of that other "penalty of Adam" beside "the seasons' difference": that man must labor to get himself food and clothing. Still, the labor is pleasant and a source of pride: "I am a true laborer: I earn that I eat, get that I wear, owe no man hate, envy no man's happiness, glad of other men's good, content with my harm; and the greatest of my pride is to see my ewes graze and my lambs suck." Arden is not a place where the laws of nature are abrogated and roses are without their thorns. If, in the world, Duke Frederick has usurped on Duke Senior, Duke Senior is aware that he has in his turn usurped upon the deer, the native burghers of the forest. If man does not slay and kill man, he kills the poor beasts. Life preys on life. Jaques, who can suck melancholy out of anything, points to the callousness that runs through nature itself as a mirror of the callousness of men. The herd abandons the wounded deer, as prosperous citizens pass with disdain the poor bankrupt, the failure. The race is to the swift. But this is Jaques's view. Orlando, demanding help for Adam, finds another image from nature:

> Then but forbear your food a little while,
> Whiles, like a doe, I go to find my fawn
> And give it food. There is a poor old man,
> Who after me hath many a weary step
> Limp'd in pure love: till he be first suffic'd,
> Oppress'd with two weak evils, age and hunger,
> I will not touch a bit.

The fact that they are both derived ultimately from folk tale is not the only thing that relates *As You Like It* to *King Lear*. Adam's somber line, "And unregarded age in corners thrown," which Quiller-Couch said might have come out of one of the greater sonnets, sums up the fate of Lear:

> Dear daughter, I confess that I am old;
> Age is unnecessary: on my knees I beg
> That you'll vouchsafe me raiment, bed, and food.

At times Arden seems a place where the same bitter lessons can be learned as Lear has to learn in his place of exile, the blasted heath. Corin's natural philosophy, which includes the knowledge that "the property of rain is to wet," is something which Lear has painfully to acquire:

When the rain came to wet me once and the wind to make me chatter, when the thunder would not peace at my bidding, there I found 'em, there I smelt 'em out. Go to, they are not men o' their words: they told me I was everything; 'tis a lie, I am not ague-proof.

He is echoing Duke Senior, who smiles at the "icy fang and churlish chiding of the winter's wind," saying:

> This is no flattery: there are counselors
> That feelingly persuade me what I am.

Amiens's lovely melancholy song:

> Blow, blow, thou winter wind,
> Thou art not so unkind
>   As man's ingratitude. . . .

> Freeze, freeze, thou bitter sky,
> That does not bite so nigh
>   As benefits forgot. . . ,

is terribly echoed in Lear's outburst:

> Blow, winds, and crack your cheeks! rage! blow!
> . . . .
> Rumble thy bellyful! Spit, fire! spout, rain!
> Nor rain, wind, thunder, fire, are my daughters:
> I tax not you, you elements, with unkindness;
> I never gave you kingdom, call'd you children. . . .

And Jaques's reflection that "All the world's a stage" becomes in Lear's mouth a cry of anguish:

> When we are born, we cry that we are come
> To this great stage of fools.

It is in Arden that Jaques presents his joyless picture of human life, passing from futility to futility and culminating in the nothingness of senility — "sans everything"; and in Arden also a bitter judgment on human relations is lightly passed in the twice repeated "Most friendship is feigning, most loving mere folly." But then one must add that hard on the heels of Jaques's melancholy conclusion Orlando enters with Adam in his arms, who, although he may be "sans teeth" and at the end of his usefulness as a servant, has, beside his store of virtue and his peace of conscience, the love of his master. And the play is full of signal instances of persons who do not forget benefits: Adam, Celia, Touchstone — not to mention the lords who chose to leave the court and follow their banished master to the forest. In a recent number of the *Shakespeare Survey* Professor Harold Jenkins has pointed out how points of view put forward by one character find contradiction or correction by another, so that the whole play is a balance of sweet against sour, of the cynical against the idealistic, and life is shown as a mingling of hard fortune and good hap. The lords who have "turned ass," "leaving their wealth and ease a stubborn will to please," are happy in their gross folly, as Orlando is in a lovesickness which he does not wish to be cured of. What Jaques has left out of his picture of man's strange eventful pilgrimage is love and companionship, sweet society, the banquet under the boughs to which Duke Senior welcomes Orlando and Adam. Although life in Arden is not wholly idyllic, and this place set apart from the world is yet touched by the world's sorrows and can be mocked at by the wordly wise, the image of life which the forest presents is irradiated by the conviction that the gay and the gentle can endure the rubs of fortune and that this earth is a place where men can find happiness in themselves and in others.

The Forest of Arden is, as has often been pointed out, a place which all the exiles from the court, except one, are only too ready to leave at the close. As, when the short midsummer night is over, the lovers emerge from the wood, in their right minds and correctly paired, and return to the palace of Theseus; and, when Prospero's magic has worked the cure, the enchanted island is left to Caliban and Ariel, and its human visitors return to Naples and Milan; so the time of holiday comes to an end in Arden. The stately masque of Hymen marks the end of this interlude in the greenwood, and announces the return to a court purged of envy and baseness. Like other comic places, Arden is a place of discovery where the truth becomes clear and where each man finds himself and his true way. This discovery of truth in comedy is made through errors and mistakings. The trial and error by which we come to knowledge of ourselves and of our world is symbolized by the disguisings which are a recurrent element in all comedy, but are particularly common in Shakespeare's. Things have, as it were, to become worse before they become better, more confused and farther from the proper pattern. By misunderstandings men come to understand, and by lies and feignings they discover truth. If Rosalind, the princess, had attempted to "cure" her lover Orlando, she might have succeeded. As Ganymede, playing Rosalind, she can try him to the limit in perfect safety, and discover that she cannot mock or flout him out of his "mad humor of love to a living humor of madness," and drive him "to forswear the full stream of the world, and to live in a nook merely monastic." By playing with him in the disguise of a boy, she discovers when she can play no more. By love of a shadow, the mere image of a charming youth, Phoebe discovers that it is better to love than to be loved and scorn one's lover. This discovery of truth by feigning, and of what is wisdom and what folly by debate, is the center of *As You Like It*. It is a play of meetings and encounters, of conversations and sets of wit: Orlando versus Jaques, Touchstone versus Corin, Rosalind versus Jaques, Rosalind versus Phoebe, and above all Rosalind versus Orlando. The truth discovered is, at one level, a very "earthy truth": Benedick's discovery that "the world must be peopled." The honest toil of Corin, the wise man of the forest, is mocked at by Touchstone as "simple sin." He brings "the ewes and the rams together" and gets his living "by the copulation of cattle." The goddess Fortune seems similarly occupied in this play: "As the ox hath his bow, the horse his curb, and the falcon her bells, so man hath his desires; and as pigeons bill, so wedlock would be nibbling." Fortune acts the role of a kindly bawd. Touchstone's marriage to Audrey is a mere coupling. Rosalind's advice to Phoebe is brutally frank: "Sell when you can, you are not for all markets." The words she uses to describe Oliver and Celia "in the very wrath of love" are hardly delicate, and after her first meeting with Orlando she confesses to her cousin that her sighs are for her "child's father." Against the natural background of the life of the forest there can be no pretense that the love of men and women can "forget the He and She." But Rosalind's behavior is at variance with her bold words. Orlando has to prove that he truly is, as he seems at first sight, the right husband for her, and show himself gentle, courteous, generous and brave, and a match for her in wit, though a poor poet. In this, the great coupling of the play, there is a marriage of true minds. The other couplings run the gamut downward from it, until we reach Touchstone's image of "a she-lamb of a twelve-month" and "a crooked-pated, old, cuckoldy ram," right at the bottom of the scale. As for the debate as to where happiness is to be found, the conclusion come to is again, like all wisdom, not very startling or original: that "minds innocent and quiet" can find happiness in court or country:

> Happy is your Grace,
> That can translate the stubbornness of fortune
> Into so quiet and so sweet a style.

And, on the contrary, those who wish to can "suck melancholy" out of anything, "as a weasel sucks eggs."

In the pairing one figure is left out. "I am for other than for dancing measures," says Jaques. Leaving the hateful sight of reveling and pastime, he betakes himself to the Duke's abandoned cave, on his way to the house of penitents where Duke Frederick has gone. The two commentators of the play are nicely contrasted. Touchstone is the parodist, Jaques the cynic. The parodist must love what he parodies. We know this from literary parody. All the best parodies are written by those who understand, because they love, the thing they mock. Only poets who love and revere the epic can write mock-heroic and the finest parody of classical tragedy comes from Housman, a great scholar. In everything that Touchstone says and does gusto, high spirits and a zest for life ring out. Essentially comic, he can adapt himself to any situation in which he may find himself. Never at a loss, he is life's master. The essence of clowning is adaptability and improvisation. The clown is never baffled and is marked by his ability to place himself at once *en rapport* with his audience, to be all things to all men, to perform the part which is required at the moment. Touchstone sustains many different roles. After hearing Silvius's lament and Rosalind's echo of it, he becomes the maudlin lover of Jane Smile; with the simple shepherd Corin he becomes the cynical and worldly-wise man of the court; with Jaques he is a melancholy moralist, musing on the power of time and the decay of all things; with the pages he acts the lordly amateur of the arts, patronizing his musicians. It is right that he should parody the rest of the cast, and join the procession into Noah's ark with his Audrey. Jaques is his opposite. He is the cynic, the person who prefers the pleasures of superiority, cold-eyed and cold-hearted. The tyrannical Duke Frederick and the cruel Oliver can be converted; but not Jaques. He likes himself as he is. He does not wish to plunge into the stream, but prefers to stand on the bank and "fish for fancies as they pass." Sir Thomas Elyot said that dancing was an image of matrimony: "In every daunse, of a most auncient custome, there daunseth together a man and a woman, holding eche other by the hande or the arme, which betokeneth concorde." There are some who will not dance, however much they are piped to, any more than they will weep when there is mourning. "In this theater of man's life," wrote Bacon, "it is reserved only for God and angels to be lookers on." Jaques arrogates to himself the divine role. He has opted out from the human condition.

It is characteristic of Shakespeare's comedies to include an element that is irreconcilable, which strikes a lightly discordant note, casts a slight shadow, and by its presence questions the completeness of the comic vision of life. In *Love's Labor's Lost* he dared to allow the news of a death to cloud the scene of revels at the close, and, through Rosaline's rebuke to Berowne, called up the image of a whole world of pain and weary suffering where "Mirth cannot move a soul in agony." The two comedies whose main action is motivated by hatred end with malice thwarted but not removed. In *The Merchant of Venice* and *Much Ado About Nothing*, Shakespeare asks us to accept the fact that the human race includes not only a good many fools and rogues but also some persons who are positively wicked, a fact which comedy usually ignores. They are prevented from doing the harm they wish to do. They are not cured of wishing to do harm. Shylock's baffled exit and Don John's flight to Messina leave the stage clear for lovers and well-wishers. The villains have to be left out of the party at the close. At the end of *Twelfth Night* the person who is left out is present. The impotent misery and fury of the humiliated Malvolio's last words, "I'll be reveng'd on the whole pack of you," call in question the whole comic scheme by which, through misunderstandings and mistakes, people come to terms with themselves and their fellows. There are some who cannot be "taught a lesson." In Malvolio pride is not purged; it is fatally wounded and embittered. It is characteristic of the delicacy of temper of *As You Like It* that its solitary figure, its outsider, Jaques, does nothing whatever to harm anyone, and is perfectly satisfied with himself and happy in his melancholy. Even more, his melancholy is a source of pleasure and amusement to others. The Duke treats him as virtually a court entertainer, and he is a natural butt for Orlando and Rosalind. Anyone in the play can put him down and feel the better for doing so. All the same his presence casts a faint shadow. His criticism of the world has its sting drawn very early by the Duke's rebuke to him as a former libertine, discharging his filth upon the world, and he is to some extent discredited before he opens his mouth by the unpleasant implication of his name. But he cannot be wholly dismissed. A certain sour distaste for life is voided through him, something most of us feel at some time or other. If he were not there to give expression to it, we might be tempted to find the picture of life in the forest too sweet. His only action is to interfere in the marriage of Touchstone and Audrey; and this he merely postpones. His effect, whenever he appears, is to deflate: the effect does not last and cheerfulness soon breaks in again. Yet as there is a scale of love, so there is a scale of sadness in the play. It runs down from the Duke's compassionate words:

> Thou seest we are not all alone unhappy:
> This wide and universal theater
> Presents more woeful pageants than the scene
> Wherein we play in,

through Rosalind's complaint "O, how full of briers is this working-day world," to Jaques's studied refusal to find anything worthy of admiration or love.

One further element in the play I would not wish to stress, because though it is pervasive it is unobtrusive: the constant, natural and easy reference to the Christian ideal of loving-kindness, gentleness, pity and humility and to the sanctions which that ideal finds in the commands and promises of religion. In this fantasy world, in which the world of our experience is imaged, this element in experience finds a place with others, and the world is shown not only as a place where we may find happiness, but as a place where both happiness and sorrow may be hallowed. The number of religious references in *As You Like It* has often been commented on, and it is striking when we consider the play's main theme. Many are of little significance and it would be humorless to enlarge upon the significance of the "old religious man" who converted Duke Frederick, or of Ganymede's "old religious uncle." But some are explicit and have a serious, unforced beauty: Orlando's appeal to outlawed men,

> If ever you have look'd on better days,
> If ever been where bells have knoll'd to church . . . ;

Adam's prayer,

> He that doth the ravens feed,
> Yea, providently caters for the sparrow,
> Be comfort to my age!

and Corin's recognition, from St. Paul, that we have to find the way to heaven by doing deeds of hospitality. These are all in character. But the God of Marriage, Hymen, speaks more solemnly than we expect and his opening words with their New Testament echo are more than conventional:

> Then is there mirth in heaven,
> When earthly things made even
> Atone together.

The appearance of the god to present daughter to father and to bless the brides and grooms turns the close into a solemnity, an image of the concord which reigns in Heaven and which Heaven blesses on earth. But this, like much else in the play, may be taken as you like it. There is no need to see any more in the god's appearance with the brides than a piece of pageantry which concludes the action with a graceful spectacle and sends the audience home contented with a very pretty play.

C. L. BARBER

The Alliance of Seriousness and Levity
in As You Like It

As You Like It is very similar in the way it moves to *A Midsummer Night's Dream* and *Love's Labour's Lost,* despite the fact that its plot is taken over almost entirely from Lodge's *Rosalynde. . . .* The reality we feel about the experience of love in the play, reality which is not in the pleasant little prose romance, comes from presenting what was sentimental extremity as impulsive extravagance and so leaving judgment free to mock what the heart embraces. The Forest of Arden, like the Wood outside Athens, is a region defined by an attitude of liberty from ordinary limitations, a festive place where the folly of romance can have its day. The first half of *As You Like It,* beginning with tyrant brother and tyrant Duke and moving out into the forest, is chiefly concerned with establishing this sense of freedom; the traditional contrast of court and country is developed in a way that is shaped by the contrast between everyday and holiday, as that antithesis has become part of Shakespeare's art and sensibility. Once we are securely in the golden world where the good Duke and "a many merry men . . . fleet the time carelessly," the pastoral motif as such drops into the background; Rosalind finds Orlando's verses in the second scene of Act III, and the rest of the play deals with love. This second movement is like a musical theme with imitative variations, developing much more tightly the sort of construction which played off Costard's and Armado's amorous affairs against those of the nobles in Navarre, and which set Bottom's imagination in juxtaposition with other shaping fantasies. The love affairs of Silvius and Phebe, Touchstone and Audrey, Orlando and Rosalind succeed one another in the easy-going sequence of scenes, while the dramatist deftly plays each off against the others.

From *Shakespeare's Festive Comedy.* Copyright © 1959 by Princeton University Press, pp. 223–238. Reprinted with minor deletions by permission of the author and the Princeton University Press.

THE LIBERTY OF ARDEN

The thing that asks for explanation about the Forest of Arden is how this version of pastoral can feel so free when the Duke and his company are so high-minded. Partly the feeling of freedom comes from release from the tension established in the first act at the jealous court:

> Now go we in content
> To liberty, and not to banishment.
>   (I.iii.139–140)

Several brief court scenes serve to keep this contrast alive. So does Orlando's entrance, sword in hand, to interrupt the Duke's gracious banquet by his threatening demand for food. Such behavior on his part is quite out of character (in Lodge he is most courteous); but his brandishing entrance gives Shakespeare occasion to resolve the attitude of struggle once again, this time by a lyric invocation of "what 'tis to pity and be pitied" (II.vii.117).

But the liberty we enjoy in Arden, though it includes relief from anxiety in brotherliness confirmed "at good men's feasts," is somehow easier than brotherliness usually is. The easiness comes from a witty redefinition of the human situation which makes conflict seem for the moment superfluous. Early in the play, when Celia and Rosalind are talking of ways of being merry by devising sports, Celia's proposal is "Let us sit and mock the good housewife Fortune from her wheel" (I.ii.34–35). The two go on with a "chase" of wit that goes "from Fortune's office to Nature's" (I.ii.43), whirling the two goddesses through many variations; distinctions between them were running in Shakespeare's mind. In Act II, the witty poetry which establishes the greenwood mood of freedom repeatedly mocks Fortune from her wheel by an act of mind which goes from Fortune to Nature:

> A fool, a fool! I met a fool i' th' forest, . . .
> Who laid him down and bask'd him in the sun
> And rail'd on Lady Fortune in good terms, . . .
> "Good morrow, fool," quoth I. "No, sir," quoth he,
> "Call me not fool till heaven hath sent me fortune."
> And then he drew a dial from his poke,
> And looking on it with lack-lustre eye,
> Says very wisely, 'It is ten o'clock.
> Thus we may see,' quoth he, 'how the world wags.
> 'Tis but an hour ago since it was nine,
> And after one more hour 'twill be eleven;
> And so, from hour to hour, we ripe and ripe,
> And then, from hour to hour, we rot and rot;
> And thereby hangs a tale.'   (II.vii.12–28)

Why does Jaques, in his stylish way, say that his lungs "began to crow like chanticleer" to hear the fool "thus moral on the time," when the moral concludes in "rot and rot"? Why do we, who are not "melancholy," feel such large and free delight? Because the fool "finds," with wonderfully bland wit, that nothing whatever happens under the aegis of Fortune. ("Fortune reigns in gifts of the world," said Rosalind at I.ii.44.) The almost tautological inevitability of nine, ten, eleven, says that all we do is ripe and ripe and rot and rot. And so there is no reason not to bask in the sun and "lose and neglect the creeping hours of time" (II.vii.112). Touchstone's "deep contemplative" moral makes the same statement as the spring song towards the close of the play: "How that a life was but a flower." When they draw the moral, the lover and his lass are only thinking of the "spring time" as they take "the present time" when "love is crowned with the prime." (The refrain mocks them a little for their obliviousness, but its tinkling "the only pretty ring time.") But Touchstone's festive gesture is *not* oblivious.

The extraordinary thing about the poised liberty of the second act is that the reduction of life to the natural and seasonal and physical works all the more convincingly as a festive release by including a recognition that the physical can be unpleasant. The good Duke, in his opening speech, can "translate the stubbornness of fortune" into a benefit: he does it by the witty shift which makes the "icy fang / And churlish chiding of the winter wind" into "counsellors / That feelingly persuade me what I am" (II.i.6–11). The two songs make the same gesture of welcoming physical pain in place of moral pain:

> Come hither, come hither, come hither!
> Here shall he see
> No enemy
> But winter and rough weather.
>   (II.v.5–8)

They are patterned on holiday drinking songs, as we have seen already in considering the Christmas refrain, "Heigh-ho, sing heigh-ho, unto the green holly," and they convey the free solidarity of a group who, since they relax in physical pleasures together, need not fear the fact that "Most friendship is feigning, most loving merely folly."

Jaques' speech on the seven ages of man, which comes at the end of Act II, just before "Blow, Blow, thou winter wind," is another version of the liberating talk about time; it expands Touchstone's "And thereby hangs a tale." The simplification "All the world's a stage," has such imaginative reach that we are as much astonished as amused, as with Touchstone's summary ripe and rot. But simplification it is, nevertheless;

quotations (and recitations) often represent it as though it were dramatist Shakespeare's "philosophy," his last word, or one of them, about
what life really comes to. To take it this way is sentimental, puts a part
in place of the whole. For it only is *one* aspect of the truth that the roles
we play in life are settled by the cycle of growth and decline. To face
this part of the truth, to insist on it, brings the kind of relief that goes
with accepting folly — indeed this speech is praise of folly, superbly gen-
eralized, praise of the folly of living in time (or is it festive abuse? the
poise is such that relish and mockery are indistinguishable). Sentimental readings ignore the wit that keeps reducing social roles to
caricatures and suggesting that meanings really are only physical relations beyond the control of mind or spirit:

> Then a soldier, . . .
> Seeking the bubble reputation
> Even in the cannon's mouth. And then the justice,
> In fair round belly with good capon lin'd . . .
> (III.vii.149–154)

Looking back at time and society in this way, we have a detachment
and sense of mastery similar to that established by Titania and Oberon's
outside view of "the human mortals" and their weather.

COUNTERSTATEMENTS

That Touchstone and Jaques should at moments turn and mock pastoral contentment is consistent with the way it is presented; their
mockery makes explicit the partiality, the displacement of normal emphasis, which is implicit in the witty advocacy of it.

> If it do come to pass
> That any man turn ass,
> Leaving his wealth and ease
> A stubborn will to please . . .
> (II.v.52–55)

The folly of going to Arden has something about it of Christian humility,
brotherliness and unworldliness ("Consider the lilies of the field . . ."),
but one can also turn it upside down by "a Greek invocation to call fools
into a circle" and find it stubbornness. Touchstone brings out another
kind of latent irony about pastoral joys when he plays the role of a dis-
contented exile from the court:

CORIN: And how like you this shepherd's life, Master Touchstone!
TOUCHSTONE: Truly, shepherd, in respect of itself, it is a good life; but in

respect that it is a shepherd's life, it is naught. In respect that it is solitary, I like it very well; but in respect that it is private, it is a very vile
life. Now in respect it is in the fields, it pleaseth me well; but in respect it
is not in the court, it is tedious. As it is a spare life, look you, it fits my
humour well; but as there is no more plenty in it, it goes much against
my stomach.

(III.ii.12–22)

Under the apparent nonsense of his self-contradictions, Touchstone mocks
the contradictory nature of the desires ideally resolved by pastoral life,
to be at once at court and in the fields, to enjoy both the fat advantages
of rank and the spare advantages of the mean and sure estate. The
humor goes to the heart of the pastoral convention and shows how very
clearly Shakespeare understood it.

The fact that he created both Jaques and Touchstone out of whole
cloth, adding them to the story as it appears in Lodge's *Rosalynde*, is
an index to what he did in dramatizing the prose romance. Lodge,
though he has a light touch, treats the idyllic material at face value. He
never makes fun of its assumptions, but stays safely within the convention, because he has no securely grounded attitude towards it, not being
sure of its relation to reality. Shakespeare scarcely changes the story at
all, but where in Lodge it is presented in the flat, he brings alive the
dimension of its relation to life as a whole. The control of this dimension
makes his version solid as well as delicate.

Although both Jaques and Touchstone are connected with the action
well enough at the level of plot, their real position is generally mediate
between the audience and something in the play, the same position
Nashe assigns to the court fool, Will Summers, in *Summer's Last Will
and Testament*. Once Jaques stands almost outside the play, when he
responds to Orlando's romantic greeting: "Good day and happiness,
dear Rosalind!" with "Nay then, God b'wi'you, and you talk in blank
verse!" (IV.i.31). Jaques' factitious melancholy, which critics have
made too much of as a "psychology," serves primarily to set him at odds
both with society and with Arden and so motivate contemplative mockery. Touchstone is put outside by his special status as a fool. As a fool,
incapable, at least for professional purposes, of doing anything right,
he is beyond the pale of normal achievements. In anything he tries to
do he is comically disabled, as, for example, in falling in love. All he
achieves is a burlesque of love. So he has none of the illusions of those
who try to be ideal, and is in a position to make a business of being
dryly objective. "Call me not fool till heaven hath sent me fortune."
Heaven sends him Audrey instead, "an ill-favour'd thing, sir, but mine
own" (V.iv.60) — not a mistress to generate illusions. In *As You Like It*
the court fool for the first time takes over the work of comic commen-

tary and burlesque from the clown of the earlier plays; in Jaques' praise of Touchstone and the corrective virtues of fooling, Shakespeare can be heard crowing with delight at his discovery. The figure of the jester, with his recognized social role and rich traditional meaning, enabled the dramatist to embody in a character and his relations with other characters the comedy's purpose of maintaining objectivity.

The satirist presents life as it is and ridicules it because it is not ideal, as we would like it to be and as it should be. Shakespeare goes the other way about it: he represents or evokes ideal life, and then makes fun of it because it does not square with life as it ordinarily is. If we look for social satire in *As You Like It,* all we find are a few set pieces about such stock figures as the traveller and the duelist. And these figures seem to be described rather to enjoy their extravagance than to rebuke their folly. Jaques, in response to a topical interest at the time when the play appeared, talks a good deal about satire, and proposes to "cleanse the foul body of th' infected world" (II.vii.60) with the fool's medicine of ridicule. But neither Jaques, the amateur fool, nor Touchstone, the professional, ever really gets around to doing the satirist's work of ridiculing life as it is, "deeds, and language, such as men do use."[1] After all, they are in Arden, not in Jonson's London: the infected body of the world is far away, out of range. What they make fun of instead is what they can find in Arden — pastoral innocence and romantic love, life as it might be, lived "in a holiday humour." Similar comic presentation of what is not ideal in man is characteristic of medieval fool humor, where the humorist, by his gift of long ears to the long-robed dignitaries, makes the point that, despite their pageant perfection, they are human too, that "stultorum numerus infinitus est." Such humor is very different from modern satire, for its basic affirmation is not man's possible perfection but his certain imperfection. It was a function of the pervasively formal and ideal cast of medieval culture, where what should be was more present to the mind than what is: the humorists' natural recourse was to burlesque the pageant of perfection, presenting it as a procession of fools, in crowns, mitres, caps, and gowns. Shakespeare's point of view was not medieval. But his clown and fool comedy is a response, a counter-movement, to artistic idealization, as medieval burlesque was a response to the ingrained idealism of the culture.

"ALL NATURE IN LOVE MORTAL IN FOLLY"

I have quoted already in the Introduction a riddling comment of Touchstone which moves from acknowledging mortality to accepting the folly of love:

[1] Ben Jonson, *Every Man in His Humour*, Prologue, l.21.

We that are true lovers run into strange capers; but as all is mortal in nature,
so is all nature in love mortal in folly.
(II.iv.53–56)

The lovers who in the second half of the play present "nature in love"
each exhibit a kind of folly. In each there is a different version of the
incongruity between reality and the illusions (in poetry, the hyperboles)
which love generates and by which it is expressed. The comic variations
are centered around the seriously-felt love of Rosalind and Orlando. The
final effect is to enhance the reality of this love by making it independent
of illusions, whose incongruity with life is recognized and laughed off.
We can see this at closer range by examining each affair in turn.

All-suffering Silvius and his tyrannical little Phebe are a bit of
Lodge's version taken over, outwardly intact, and set in a wholly new
perspective. A "courting eglogue" between them, in the mode of Lodge,
is exhibited almost as a formal spectacle, with Corin for presenter and
Rosalind and Celia for audience. It is announced as

> a pageant truly play'd
> Between the pale complexion of true love
> And the red glow of scorn and proud disdain.
> (III.iv.55–57)

What we then watch is played "truly" — according to the best current
convention: Silvius, employing a familiar gambit, asks for pity; Phebe
refuses to believe in love's invisible wound, with exactly the literal-
mindedness about hyperbole which the sonneteers imputed to their
mistresses. In Lodge's version, the unqualified Petrarchan sentiments of
the pair are presented as valid and admirable. Shakespeare lets us feel
the charm of the form; but then he has Rosalind break up their pretty
pageant. She reminds them that they are nature's creatures, and that
love's purposes are contradicted by too absolute a cultivation of romantic
liking or loathing: "I must tell you friendly in your ear, / Sell when
you can! you are not for all markets" (III.v.59–60). Her exaggerated
downrightness humorously underscores the exaggerations of conventional sentiment. And Shakespeare's treatment breaks down Phebe's
stereotyped attitudes to a human reality: he lightly suggests an adolescent perversity underlying her resistance to love. The imagery she
uses in disputing with Silvius is masterfully squeamish, at once pre-
occupied with touch and shrinking from it:

> 'Tis pretty, sure, and very probable
> That eyes, which are the frail'st and softest things,
> Who shut their coward gates on atomies,

> Should be call'd tyrants, butchers, murtherers!
> . . . lean but upon a rush,
> The cicatrice and capable impressure
> Thy palm some moment keeps; but now mine eyes,
> Which I have darted at thee, hurt thee not, . . .
>   (III.v.11–25)

Rosalind, before whom this resistance melts, appears in her boy's disguise "like a ripe sister," and the qualities Phebe picks out to praise are feminine. She has, in effect, a girlish crush on the femininity which shows through Rosalind's disguise; the aberrant affection is happily got over when Rosalind reveals her identity and makes it manifest that Phebe has been loving a woman. "Nature to her bias drew in that" is the comment in *Twelfth Night* when Olivia is fortunately extricated from a similar mistaken affection.

Touchstone's affair with Audrey complements the spectacle of exaggerated sentiment by showing love reduced to its lowest common denominator, without any sentiment at all. The fool is detached, objective and resigned when the true-blue lover should be

> All made of passion, and all made of wishes,
> All adoration, duty, and observance.
>   (V.ii.101–102)

He explains to Jaques his reluctant reasons for getting married:

JAQUES: Will you be married, motley?

TOUCHSTONE: As the ox hath his bow, sir, the horse his curb, and the falcon her bells, so man hath his desires; and as pigeons bill, so wedlock would be nibbling.

                                                    (III.iii.79–83)

This reverses the relation between desire and its object, as experienced by the other lovers. They are first overwhelmed by the beauty of their mistresses, then impelled by that beauty to desire them. With Touchstone, matters go the other way about: he discovers that man has his troublesome desires, as the horse his curb; then he decides to cope with the situation by marrying Audrey:

> Come, sweet Audrey.
> We must be married, or we must live in bawdry.
>   (III.iii.98–99)

Like all the motives which Touchstone acknowledges, this priority of desire to attraction is degrading and humiliating. One of the hall-marks of chivalric and Petrarchan idealism is, of course, the high valuation of the lover's mistress, the assumption that his desire springs entirely from her beauty. This attitude of the poets has contributed to that progressively-increasing respect for women so fruitful in modern culture. But to assume that only one girl will do is, after all, an extreme, an ideal attitude: the other half of the truth, which lies in wait to mock sublimity, is instinct — the need of a woman, even if she be an Audrey, because "as pigeons bill, so wedlock would be nibbling." As Touchstone put it on another occasion:

> If the cat will after kind,
> So be sure will Rosalinde.
> (III.ii.109–110)

The result of including in Touchstone a representative of what in love is unromantic is not, however, to undercut the play's romance: on the contrary, the fool's cynicism, or one-sided realism, forestalls the cynicism with which the audience might greet a play where his sort of realism had been ignored. We have a sympathy for his downright point of view, not only in connection with love but also in his acknowledgment of the vain and self-gratifying desires excluded by pastoral humility; he embodies the part of ourselves which resists the play's reigning idealism. But he does not do so in a fashion to set himself up in opposition to the play. Romantic commentators construed him as "Hamlet in motely," a devastating critic. They forgot, characteristically, that he is ridiculous: he makes his attitudes preposterous when he values rank and comfort above humility, or follows biology rather than beauty. In laughing at him, we reject the tendency in ourselves which he for the moment represents. The net effect of the fool's part is thus to consolidate the hold of the serious themes by exorcising opposition. The final Shakespearean touch is to make the fool aware that in humiliating himself he is performing a public service. He goes through his part with an irony founded on the fact (and it is a fact) that he is only making manifest the folly which others, including the audience, hide from themselves.

Romantic participation in love and humorous detachment from its follies, the two polar attitudes which are balanced against each other in the action as a whole, meet and are reconciled in Rosalind's personality. Because she remains always aware of love's illusions while she herself is swept along by its deepest currents, she possesses as an attribute of character the power of combining wholehearted feeling and undistorted judgment which gives the play its value. She plays the mocking reveller's role which Berowne played in *Love's Labour's Lost*, with the advantage of disguise. Shakespeare exploits her disguise to permit her to furnish the humorous commentary on her own ardent love affair, thus keeping comic and serious actions going at the same time. In her pretended role of saucy shepherd youth, she can mock at romance and bur-lesque its gestures while playing the game of putting Orlando through his paces as a suitor, to "cure" him of love. But for the audience, her disguise is transparent, and through it they see the very ardor which she mocks. When, for example, she stages a gayly overdone take-off of the conventional impatience of the lover, her own real impatience comes through the burlesque; yet the fact that she makes fun of exaggerations of the feeling conveys an awareness that it has limits, that there is a difference between romantic hyperbole and human nature:

> ORLANDO: For these two hours, Rosalind, I will leave thee.
> ROSALIND: Alas, dear love, I cannot lack thee two hours!
> ORLANDO: I must attend the Duke at dinner. By two o'clock I will be with thee again.
> ROSALIND: Ay, go your ways, go your ways! I knew what you would prove. My friends told me as much, and I thought no less. That flattering tongue of yours won me. 'Tis but one cast away, and so, come death! Two o'clock is your hour?
>
> (IV.i.181–190)

One effect of this indirect, humorous method of conveying feeling is that Rosalind is not committed to the conventional language and atti-tudes of love, loaded as these inevitably are with sentimentality. Silvius and Phebe are her foils in this: they take their conventional language and their conventional feelings perfectly seriously, with nothing in reserve. As a result they seem naïve and rather trivial. They are no more than what they say, until Rosalind comes forward to realize their personalities for the audience by suggesting what they humanly are be-neath what they romantically think themselves. By contrast, the hero-ine in expressing her own love conveys by her humorous tone a valuation of her sentiments, and so realizes her own personality for herself, without being indebted to another for the favor. She uses the convention where Phebe, being unaware of its exaggerations, abuses it, and Silvius, equally naïve about hyperbole, lets it abuse him. This control of tone is one of the great contributions of Shakespeare's comedy to his dramatic art as a whole. The discipline of comedy in controlling the humorous poten-tialities of a remark enables the dramatist to express the relation of a speaker to his lines, including the relation of naïveté. The focus of attention is not on the outward action of saying something but on the shifting, uncrystallized life which motivates what is said.

The particular feeling of headlong delight in Rosalind's encounters with Orlando goes with the prose of these scenes, a medium which can put imaginative effects of a very high order to the service of humor and wit. The comic prose of this period is first developed to its full range in Falstaff's part, and steals the show for Benedict and Beatrice in

Much Ado About Nothing. It combines the extravagant linguistic reach
of the early clowns' prose with the sophisticated wit which in the earlier
plays was usually cast, less flexibly, in verse. Highly patterned, it is
built up of balanced and serial clauses, with everything linked together
by alliteration and kicked along by puns. Yet it avoids a stilted, Euphu-
istic effect because regular patterns are set going only to be broken to
underscore humor by asymmetry. The speaker can rock back and forth
on antitheses, or climb "a pair of stairs" (V.ii.42) to a climax, then slow
down meaningly, or stop dead, and so punctuate a pithy reduction,
bizarre exaggeration or broad allusion. T. S. Eliot has observed that we
often forget that it was Shakespeare who wrote the greatest prose in the
language. Some of it is in *As You Like It*. His control permits him to
convey the constant shifting of attitude and point of view which expresses Rosalind's excitement and her poise. Such writing, like the
brushwork and line of great painters, is in one sense everything. But the
whole design supports each stroke, as each stroke supports the whole
design.

The expression of Rosalind's attitude towards being in love, in the
great scene of disguised wooing, fulfills the whole movement of the play.
The climax comes when Rosalind is able, in the midst of her golden
moment, to look beyond it and mock its illusions, including the master
illusion that love is an ultimate and final experience, a matter of life and
death. Ideally, love should be final, and Orlando is romantically convinced that his is so, so that he would die if Rosalind refused him. But
Rosalind humorously corrects him, from behind her page's disguise:

> . . . Am I not your Rosalind?
>
> ORLANDO: I take some joy to say you are, because I would be talking of her.
> ROSALIND: Well, in her person, I say I will not have you.
> ORLANDO: Then, in mine own person, I die.
> ROSALIND: No, faith, die by attorney. The poor world is almost six thousand
> years old, and in all this time there was not any man died in his own
> person, videlicet, in a love cause. Troilus had his brains dash'd out with
> a Grecian club; yet he did what he could to die before, and he is one of
> the patterns of love. Leander, he would have liv'd many a fair year
> though Hero had turn'd nun, if it had not been for a hot midsummer
> night; for (good youth) he went but forth to wash him in the Helles-
> pont, and being taken with the cramp, was drown'd; and the foolish
> chroniclers of that age found it was "Hero of Sestos." But these are all
> lies. Men have died from time to time, and worms have eaten them, but
> not for love.
> ORLANDO: I would not have my right Rosalind of this mind, for I protest
> her frown might kill me.
> ROSALIND: By this hand, it will not kill a fly!
>
> (IV.i.90–108)

A note almost of sadness comes through Rosalind's mockery towards the end. It is not sorrow that men die from time to time, but that they do not die for love, that love is not so final as romance would have it. For a moment we experience as pathos the tension between feeling and judgment which is behind all the laughter. The same pathos of objectivity is expressed by Chaucer in the sad smile of Pandarus as he contemplates the illusions of Troilus' love. But in *As You Like It* the mood is dominant only in the moment when the last resistance of feeling to judgment is being surmounted: the illusions thrown up by feeling are mastered by laughter and so love is reconciled with judgment. This resolution is complete by the close of the wooing scene. As Rosalind rides the crest of a wave of happy fulfillment (for Orlando's behavior to the pretended Rosalind has made it perfectly plain that he loves the real one) we find her describing with delight, almost in triumph, not the virtues of marriage, but its fallibility:

> Say "a day" without the "ever." No, no, Orlando! Men are April when they woo, December when they wed. Maids are May when they are maids, but the sky changes when they are wives.
>
> (IV.i.146–150)

Ordinarily, these would be strange sentiments to proclaim with joy at such a time. But as Rosalind says them, they clinch the achievement of the humor's purpose. (The wry, retarding change from the expected cadence at "but the sky changes" is one of those brush strokes that fulfill the large design.) Love has been made independent of illusions without becoming any the less intense; it is therefore inoculated against life's unromantic contradictions. To emphasize by humor the limitations of the experience has become a way of asserting its reality. The scenes which follow move rapidly and deftly to complete the consummation of the love affairs on the level of plot. The treatment becomes more and more frankly artificial, to end with a masque. But the lack of realism in presentation does not matter, because a much more important realism in our attitude towards the substance of romance has been achieved already by the action of the comedy.

In writing of Marvell and the metaphysical poets, T. S. Eliot spoke of an "alliance of levity and seriousness (by which the seriousness is intensified)." What he has said about the contribution of wit to this poetry is strikingly applicable to the function of Shakespeare's comedy in *As You Like It:* that wit conveys "a recognition, implicit in the expression of every experience, of other kinds of experience which are possible."[2] The likeness does not consist simply in the fact that the wit of certain

2 *Selected Essays, 1917–1932* (New York, 1932), pp. 255 and 262.

of Shakespeare's characters at times is like the wit of the metaphysicals. The crucial similarity is in the way the humor functions in the play as a whole to implement a wider awareness, maintaining proportion where less disciplined and coherent art falsifies by presenting a part as though it were the whole. The dramatic form is very different from the lyric: Shakespeare does not have or need the sustained, inclusive poise of metaphysical poetry when, at its rare best, it fulfills Cowley's ideal:

> In a true piece of Wit all things must be
> Yet all things there agree.

The dramatist tends to show us one thing at a time, and to realize that one thing, in its moment, to the full; his characters go to extremes, comical as well as serious; and no character, not even a Rosalind, is in a position to see all around the play and so be completely poised, for if this were so the play would cease to be dramatic. Shakespeare, moreover, has an Elizabethan delight in extremes for their own sake, beyond the requirements of his form and sometimes damaging to it, an expansiveness which was subordinated later by the seventeenth century's conscious need for coherence. But his extremes, where his art is at its best, are balanced in the whole work. He uses his broad-stroked, wide-swung comedy for the same end that the seventeenth-century poets achieved by their wire-drawn wit. In Silvius and Phebe he exhibits the ridiculous (and perverse) possibilities of that exaggerated romanticism which the metaphysicals so often mocked in their serious love poems. In Touchstone he includes a representative of just those aspects of love which are not romantic, hypostatizing as a character what in direct lyric expression would be an irony:

> Love's not so pure and abstract as they use
> To say who have no mistress but their muse.

By Rosalind's mockery a sense of love's limitations is kept alive at the very moments when we most feel its power:

> But at my back I always hear
> Time's wing'd chariot hurrying near.

The fundamental common characteristic is that the humor is not directed at "some outside sentimentality or stupidity," but is an agency for achieving proportion of judgment and feeling about a seriously felt experience.

As You Like It seems to me the most perfect expression Shakespeare or anyone else achieved of a poise which was possible because a traditional way of living connected different kinds of experience to each other.

HAROLD C. GODDARD

Rosalind and Touchstone

WHEN I READ the commentators on Touchstone, I rub my eyes. You
would think to hear most of them that he is a genuinely wise and witty
man and that Shakespeare so considered him. That Shakespeare knew
he could pass him off for that in a theater may be agreed. What he is is
another matter. A "dull fool" Rosalind calls him on one occasion. "O
noble fool! a worthy fool!" says Jaques on another. It is easy to guess
with which of the two Shakespeare came nearer to agreeing. The
Elizabethan groundlings had to have their clown. At his best, Touchstone is merely one more and one of the most inveterate of the author's
word-jugglers, and at his worst (as a wit) precisely what Rosalind called
him. What he is at his worst as a man justifies still harsher characterization.

In her first speech after he enters the play in the first act, Rosalind
describes him as "the cutter-off of Nature's wit," and his role abun-
dantly justifies her judgment. "Thou speakest wiser than thou art ware
of," she says to him on another occasion, and as if expressly to prove the
truth of what she says, Touchstone obligingly replies, "Nay, I shall ne'er
be ware of mine own wit till I break my shins against it." Which is
plainly Shakespeare's conscious and Touchstone's unconscious way of
stating that his wit is low. And his manners are even lower, as he shows
when he first accosts Corin and Rosalind rebukes him for his rude tone:

> TOUCH.:   Holla, you clown!
> Ros.: Peace, fool; he's not thy kinsman.
> COR.:   Who calls?
> TOUCH.: Your betters, sir.
> COR.:   Else are they very wretched.
> Ros.: Peace, I say. Good even to you, friend.

Nothing could show more succinctly Rosalind's "democracy" in contrast

Reprinted from *The Meaning of Shakespeare* by Harold C. Goddard by permission of The
University of Chicago Press. Copyright 1951 by The University of Chicago Press. This selection represents part IV of the essay "As You Like It." Title provided by the present editor.

to Touchstone's snobbery. (No wonder the people thought highly of her, as they did of Hamlet.) The superiority in wisdom of this "clown" to the man who condescends to him comes out, as we might predict it would, a little later.

> TOUCH.: Wast ever in court, shepherd?
> COR.: No, truly.
> TOUCH.: Then thou art damned.
> COR.: Nay, I hope.
> TOUCH.: Truly, thou art damned, like an ill-roasted egg all on one side.

It is an almost invariable rule in Shakespeare, as it is in life, that when one man damns another, even in jest, he unconsciously utters judgment on himself, and the rest of the scene, like Touchstone's whole role, is dedicated to showing that he himself is his own ill-roasted egg, all "wit" and word-play and nothing else.

> COR.: For not being at court? Your reason.
> TOUCH.: Why, if thou never wast at court, thou never sawest good manners [*We have just had, and are now having, a sample of the manners of this "courtier" who greeted Corin as a "clown."*]; if thou never sawest good manners, then thy manners must be wicked; and wickedness is sin, and sin is damnation. Thou art in a parlous state, shepherd.

Corin may be a "silly" shepherd but he is not taken in by this silly verbal legerdemain. He stands up to his "better" stoutly:

> COR.: Not a whit, Touchstone: those that are good manners at the court, are as ridiculous in the country as the behaviour of the country is most mockable at the court,

and he illustrates by pointing out that the habit of kissing hands at court would be uncleanly among shepherds. Whereupon, as we might expect, Touchstone, forgetting his own rule that he who calls himself wise is a fool, cries "Learn of the wise," and descends to an even lower level of sophistry than before. Corin, sensing that it is futile to argue with such a man, refuses to continue, but refuses with a courtesy at the opposite pole from Touchstone's rudeness, and we suddenly realize that Shakespeare has contrived the whole episode as a refutation on the plane of life of the conclusion for which Touchstone is contending: that good manners are impossible for a countryman.

> COR.: You have too courtly a wit for me; I'll rest.

In reply to which we have an example of courtly wit and manners:

TOUCH.: Wilt thou rest damned? God help thee, shallow man!

Shallow man! the best possible characterization of Touchstone himself
at the moment. And as if to show by way of contrast what a deep man
is, Shakespeare lets Corin condense his life into a sentence which, if a
sentence ever was, is a perfect blend of modesty and pride:

> COR.: Sir, I am a true labourer: I earn that I eat, get that I wear, owe no
> man hate, envy no man's happiness, glad of other men's good, content
> with my harm; and the greatest of my pride is to see my ewes graze and
> my lambs suck.

It is one of the tersest and one of the finest "creeds" to be found anywhere in Shakespeare, at the farthest possible remove from Touchstone's
own which Jaques overheard and quoted. And with all his "wit" the
only thing Touchstone can think up by way of retort is the taunt that
Corin by his own confession is a "bawd" because, forsooth, he makes
his living by the multiplication of his stock. A Hottentot would be
ashamed of such reasoning, and for the jocosity of it, it is close to
Touchstone's "low," which is saying a good deal. To the crass animality
and ribaldry of this courtier Shakespeare, with another of his sudden
switches, instantly opposes the "sanctity" of the man whose very kisses
are like "the touch of holy bread": Rosalind, as Ganymede, enters reading snatches of the verses her lover has been hanging or carving on the
trees.

> Her worth, being mounted on the wind,
> Through all the world bears Rosalind,

verses which Touchstone, as we would expect, proceeds to parody in
such choice lines as:

> If the cat will after kind,
> So be sure will Rosalind.

What wonder that Rosalind rebukes the man as a "dull fool" and tells
him that, like a medlar, he will be rotten ere he is ripe. The simile is a
manifest double allusion on Shakespeare's part, first, to Touchstone's
own "ill-roasted egg" (the same idea under another image), and, second,
to Touchstone's summary of human life:

> And so, from hour to hour we ripe and ripe,
> And then from hour to hour we rot and rot.

If we know anything about the man who through the mouth of Edgar in

King Lear declared that "Ripeness is all," we know what he must have thought of this philosophy of Touchstone's. He must have thought it rotten — rotten not in any modern colloquial sense of the term but rotten in the full implication of the horticultural metaphor.

But even with all this mauling, Shakespeare is not done with Touchstone. Having demonstrated to the hilt that his wit instead of sharpening has dulled his wits, he proceeds to show that his wit has also withered his heart. It is in his interlude with Audrey that we see Touchstone at his moral nadir. It will be said, of course, that this episode is pure farce and that to take it seriously is to show lack of humor. The objection need disturb nobody but the man who makes it. For of all the strange things about this man William Shakespeare one of the most remarkable is the fact that he could contrive no scene so theatrical, no stage effect so comic or dialogue so nonsensical, as to protect himself from the insertion right in the midst of it of touches of nature scientific in their veracity. Such was the grip that truth seems to have had on him.

Audrey is generally dismissed as a country wench expressly set up as a butt for Touchstone. And a theater audience can be duly counted on to roar with laughter at her. She is indeed just a goatherd, plain in appearance (though doubtless not as plain as Touchstone would make out) and so unlettered that most words of more than one syllable bewilder her simple wits. Touchstone's literary and mythological puns and allusions are naturally lost on her. But the attentions of this stranger from the court have awakened unwonted emotions and aspirations in her breast, and nothing could be clearer than her desire to be modest and true and pure. Love is the great leveler as well as the great lifter, and Audrey, perhaps for the first time in her life, feels that even she may have a place in God's world. And this is the way Touchstone deals with the emotion he has awakened:

TOUCH.: Truly, I would the gods had made thee poetical.
AUD.: I do not know what "poetical" is. Is it honest in deed and word? Is it a true thing?
TOUCH.: No, truly, for the truest poetry is the most feigning; and lovers are given to poetry, and what they swear in poetry may be said as lovers they do feign.
AUD.: Do you wish then that the gods had made me poetical?
TOUCH.: I do, truly; for thou swearest to me thou art honest; now, if thou wert a poet, I might have some hope thou didst feign.
AUD.: Would you not have me honest?
TOUCH.: No, truly, unless thou wert hard-favour'd; for honesty coupled to beauty is to have honey a sauce to sugar.
JAQ.: (*Aside*): A material fool.
AUD.: Well, I am not fair, and therefore I pray the gods make me honest.

TOUCH.: Truly, and to cast away honesty upon a foul slut were to put good meat into an unclean dish.

AUD.: I am not a slut, though I thank the gods I am foul.

TOUCH.: Well, praised be the gods for thy foulness! sluttishness may come hereafter.

As "theater" this is doubtless what a modern director might call "sure-fire stuff." As life it comes close to being the sin against the Holy Ghost. Touchstone of course is planning to marry Audrey ("to take that that no man else will") and abandon her as soon as he is sick of his bargain, and when Sir Oliver Martext, a marrying parson, enters, he is ready to go ahead with the ceremony then and there. Jaques, who has been eavesdropping, coming forward offers at first to "give the woman." But on second thought the scandalous procedure is too much for even him to stomach and he rebukes Touchstone roundly for his conduct, about the best thing Jaques does in the play:

> And will you, being a man of your breeding, be married under a bush like a beggar? Get you to church, and have a good priest that can tell you what marriage is.

But a good priest and a binding marriage are precisely what Touchstone does not want.

Later, Shakespeare treats us to a little encounter between Touchstone and William, the forest youth who "lays claim" to Audrey. Setting out to make a fool of him, Touchstone asks him if he is wise.

WILL.: Ay, sir, I have a pretty wit.

TOUCH.: Why, thou sayest well. I do now remember a saying, "The fool doth think he is wise, but the wise man knows himself to be a fool."

But in that case Touchstone stands condemned as a fool by his own rule, for about twenty lines back in this same scene he had said, "By my troth, we that have good wits have much to answer for." And about ten lines farther on he again convicts himself by his own rule even more convincingly:

> TOUCH.: You do love this maid?
> WILL.: I do, sir.
> TOUCH.: Give me your hand. Art thou learned?
> WILL.: No, sir.
> TOUCH.: Then learn this of me. . . .

Whereupon, addressing William as "you clown," he announces that he, Touchstone, is the man who is to marry Audrey, and orders his rival on pain of death to abandon her company, meanwhile drowning him under such a flood of unfamiliar words that the bewildered youth is only too glad to decamp. "Oh, but Touchstone's threats to kill are just jest," it will be said, "and his superiority and condescension just mock-heroics and mock-pedantics. Again you are guilty of taking seriously what is mere fooling, making a mountain out of a molehill of the text, and treating William as if he were a real human being instead of the theatrical puppet that he is." (As if Shakespeare did not make even his most minor characters human beings!) Granted that to Touchstone the whole thing is a huge joke; that does not make his torrent of talk any less perplexing or menacing to William, nor the theft of Audrey any less mean or immoral. It is merely a consummation of what this man in motley has revealed throughout: his snobbery and bad manners, and ultimately his hard heart. Touchstone, if you insist, is making a fool of this rustic simpleton, William. It is another William who is making a fool of Touchstone.

So even the tormented comes off better than the tormentor. Indeed nearly everybody in the play does who comes in contact with Touchstone. "A touchstone," says the dictionary, is "a black siliceous stone used to test the purity of gold and silver by the streak left on the stone when rubbed by the metal." Not precious itself, it reveals preciousness in what touches it. That seems to be precisely the function assigned to Touchstone in this play, so perhaps its author knew what he was doing when he named him. Near the end two of the banished Duke's pages enter and Touchstone asks them for a song. They comply with his request by singing

It was a lover and his lass,

and when they are done Touchstone rewards them by remarking, "Truly, young gentlemen, though there was no great matter in the ditty, yet the note was very untuneable." "You are deceived, sir," the First Page protests, "we kept time; we lost not our time." "By my troth, yes," Touchstone persists, "I count it but time lost to hear such a foolish song." Here again Shakespeare lets Touchstone judge himself in judging others, for though as manikin he will doubtless long continue to entertain the crowd in the theater, as man he is even more empty of both matter and music than the foolish song he counts it time lost to listen to. Touchstone is "wit" without love.

JOHN PALMER

Touchstone Defended

IN MOST OF Shakespeare's comedies there is a character who stands, as it were, at the centre. To get a clear view of the composition as a whole we must take up our position as near as possible beside him.

In *Love's Labour's Lost* we found our point of reference for the comic values of the play in Berowne. In *A Midsummer Night's Dream* it may be said concerning Bottom that "if he come not, the play is marred." For *As You Like It* the author has named his own Touchstone. It is as though Shakespeare, setting out for Arden, where so many excellent poets have lost themselves in affected sentiment, mislaid their common sense in refining upon their sensibility and, in their self-conscious pursuit of nature, found themselves grasping a pale misfeatured shadow, had determined in advance to take with him a guide who should keep him in the path of sanity. Touchstone puts all things and every person in the play, including himself, to the comic test. Entering Arden with Touchstone you cannot go astray or mistake the wood for the trees.

It is his function to "speak wisely what wise men do foolishly" and he loses no time about it. We are to accept him at once as no respecter of false persons:

TOUCHSTONE: Mistress, you must come away to your father.

CELIA: Were you made the messenger?

TOUCHSTONE: No, by mine honour, but I was bid to come for you.

ROSALIND: Where learned you that oath, fool?

TOUCHSTONE: Of a certain knight, that swore by his honour they were good pancakes, and swore by his honour the mustard was naught: now I'll stand to it, the pancakes were naught and the mustard was good, and yet was not the knight forsworn.

CELIA: How prove you that, in the great heap of your knowledge?

ROSALIND: Ay, marry, now unmuzzle your wisdom.

From *Political and Comic Characters of Shakespeare* (London: Macmillan & Company Ltd.; New York: St. Martin's Press, 1961), pp. 35–40. First edition 1945. This selection from the essay "Touchstone" is reprinted by permission of the St. Martin's Press. Title provided by the present editor.

TOUCHSTONE: Stand you both forth now: stroke your chins, and swear by your beards that I am a knave.

CELIA: By our beards (if we had them) thou art.

TOUCHSTONE: By my knavery (if I had it) then I were: but if you swear by that that is not, you are not forsworn:

We are next to observe that this Touchstone has a lively sense of the fitness of things. Le Beau enters to tell the ladies of much good sport — how Charles, the wrestler, has broken the ribs of three proper young men, of excellent growth and presence:

TOUCHSTONE: But what is the sport, monsieur, that the ladies have lost?

LE BEAU: Why, this that I speak of.

TOUCHSTONE: Thus men may grow wiser every day. It is the first time that ever I heard breaking of ribs was sport for ladies.

We are to esteem him also as a loyal servant who, without any illusions as to the sequel, is ready at a word to "go along o'er the wide world" with his mistress. This is no merely incidental touch. That Touchstone should set out in sturdy devotion, with an agreeably romantic expectation, is a fact essential to our appreciation of his quality. *His* part in the comedy is to shed the light of reality and common sense upon its fanciful figures and diversions. To play such a part he must be either a true cynic or one that affects his cynicism to mask a fundamentally genial spirit. Now a true cynic would be out of place in the forest of Arden. So Touchstone must be a thoroughly good fellow at heart. His brain may be as dry as the remainder biscuit after a voyage but he must be essentially a genial spirit. His acidity must be no more than skin-deep. He will see things as they are but without malice. He will have a keen flair for absurdity in people and things — not least for his own infirmities. He will, moreover, bring all things to the test of action, and the climax of *his* comedy will be to marry a slut so that he may embrace in reality the simple life which for his companions is no more than a holiday affectation.

How characteristic is his entry into the pastoral pleasaunce:

ROSALIND: O Jupiter! How weary are my spirits!

TOUCHSTONE: I care not for my spirits, if my legs were not weary.

ROSALIND: Well, this is the forest of Arden.

TOUCHSTONE: Ay, now am I in Arden, the more fool I. When I was at home, I was in a better place, but travellers must be content.

This is wholesome correction and it comes most aptly between a touching scene in which Adam displays "the constant service of the antique world," and our first encounter with Silvius and Corin — a young man and an old in solemn talk. Note, too, how he pricks the bladder of sentiment, not by rejecting its appeal, but by claiming a share in its manifestations. The love of Silvius for Phebe and of Rosalind for Orlando prompts him to declare: "We that are true lovers run into strange capers; but as all is mortal in nature, so is all nature in love mortal in folly"; and he is driven to remember — nor do we doubt the fidelity of the reminiscence — his own love for Jane Smile and the kissing of her batler and the cow's dugs that her pretty chopt hands had milked. All Touchstone is in that little speech — his quaint pretension to philosophy and a capacity for romance, rooted in nature but aware of its own excess. Jane Smile's hands were pretty but the eye of the realist could not avoid noticing that they were chopt. . . .

Even the incomparable Rosalind, whose tide of wit and flush of love set her above any need of correction by the comic spirit, must be brought to the test if only to show how triumphantly she survives it. Orlando's rhymes are redeemed by the sincerity of his passion. But some of them have more feet than the verses will bear and the feet are lame. Indeed they are very tedious homilies of love, and all this she merrily declares. And Touchstone must also have his say. It is he who, on his author's behalf, must intimate very clearly that poetasters of the pastoral school are more deserving of mockery than imitation:

ROSALIND: 'From the east to western Ind,
    No jewel is like Rosalind.
    Her worth being mounted on the wind,
    Through all the world bears Rosalind.
    All the pictures fairest lined
    Are but black to Rosalind.
    Let no face be kept in mind
    But the fair of Rosalind.'
TOUCHSTONE: I'll rhyme you so eight years together, dinners, and suppers, and sleeping-hours excepted: it is the right butter-women's rank to market.
ROSALIND: Out, fool!
TOUCHSTONE: For a taste. . . .
    If a hart do lack a hind,
    Let him seek out Rosalind:
    If the cat will after kind,
    So be sure will Rosalind:
    Wintered garments must be lined,
    So must slender Rosalind.
    They that reap must sheaf and bind,
    Then to cart with Rosalind.
    Sweetest nut hath sourest rind,

Such a nut is Rosalind.
He that sweetest rose will find,
Must find love's prick and Rosalind.
This is the very false gallop of verses. Why do you infect yourself with
them?
ROSALIND: Peace, you dull fool! I found them on a tree.
TOUCHSTONE: Truly, the tree yields bad fruit.

Orlando's poem is itself a parody. Touchstone's is a parody twice over.
Again he plays for us the author's trick. The pastoral exercise is pleasant
in itself but still more pleasant for being so easily mocked.

Touchstone's place in the comedy is ridiculed as much by what he
may do as by what his author carefully disallows. It is true that he
makes antic hay of Orlando's verses and is reminded of Jane Smile on
seeing his mistress in love, but he is not permitted to intrude into the
courtship of Rosalind and Orlando. Rosalind stands in no need of
correction save by her own true heart and wholesome intelligence. She
is her own Touchstone and carries her own comedy in person. . . .

The supreme test for Touchstone is his encounter with Jaques. But
it is well, before we examine an incident which will determine our outlook on the entire comedy, to become more intimately acquainted with
the man himself. Shakespeare affords us an opportunity in the episode
of Touchstone's courting of Audrey. Here we behold the man who has
no illusions concerning nature frankly responding to her call. The
others merely trifle with her; Touchstone sees, hears and obeys:

As the ox hath his bow, sir, the horse his curb, and the falcon her bells,
so man hath his desires; and as pigeons bill, so wedlock would be nibbling.

He has found rich honesty, dwelling like a miser in a poor house, "as
your pearl in your foul oyster," and, having found it, has the courage
of his convictions and will not let it go. His wooing of Audrey is at the
same time a burlesque and a true reflection in nature of the three romantic courtships among which it intrudes. There is conscious irony in his
claim to be pressing in "among the rest of the country copulatives, to
swear and to forswear, according as marriage binds and blood breaks,"
for none knows better than Touchstone himself that he alone is paying
a genuine tribute to the ancient gods of the forest. His surrender to the
great god, Pan, is the more complete, and certainly the more entirely
comic, for his being clearly aware of what he is doing. He is still the
courtier and he must still be flouting — even at the "poor virgin, sir, an
ill-favoured thing, sir, but mine own." He will go so far as to suggest
that "not being well-married, it will be a good excuse hereafter to leave
my wife." But all these floutings are superficial. Touchstone's comedy,

in fact, shows all the rest of the comedy in reverse. His wooing of Audrey is irony in action. Orlando, Rosalind, Silvius, Phebe and the rest affect their pastoral simplicity but remain entirely civilised. Touchstone affects his urbanity but is at heart a truly natural philosopher None knows better than he what he is doing, for it is of the essence of his character to see himself as he sees everyone else in the play in detachment:

> A man may, if he were of a fearful heart, stagger in this attempt; for here we have no temple but the wood, no assembly but horn-beasts. But what though? Courage!

He begins his courtship with a double pun and a sidelong mockery of the whole pastoral outfit:

> I am here with thee and thy goats, as the most capricious poet, honest Ovid, was among the Goths —

but his deeds in plain English speak louder than the word-play in Latin.

Now that we begin to know our Touchstone we can have no doubt of what really happened upon his first encounter with Jaques. It is Jaques himself who describes the meeting:

> A fool, a fool! I met a fool i' th' forest,
> A motley fool — a miserable world! —
> As I do live by food, I met a fool,
> Who laid him down and basked him in the sun,
> And railed on Lady Fortune in good terms,
> In good set terms, and yet a motley fool.
> 'Good morrow, fool,' quoth I: 'No, sir,' quoth he,
> 'Call me not fool till heaven hath sent me fortune.'
> And then he drew a dial from his poke,
> And looking on it with lack-lustre eye,
> Says very wisely, "It is ten o'clock:
> Thus we may see", quoth he, "how the world wags:
> 'Tis but an hour ago since it was nine,
> And after one hour more 'twill be eleven,
> And so from hour to hour, we ripe, and ripe,
> And then from hour to hour, we rot, and rot —
> And thereby hangs a tale.". . . When I did hear
> The motley fool thus moral on the time,
> My lungs began to crow like chanticleer,
> That fools should be so deep-contemplative;
> And I did laugh, sans intermission,
> An hour by his dial. . . . O noble fool!
> O worthy fool! Motley's the only wear.

Jaques relates how he has been amusing himself with a fool, but Touchstone, we perceive, has been amusing himself — and more to the purpose — with a philosopher. While Jaques was laughing at the fool, the fool was taking his measure and pulling his leg. Here Touchstone saw at once was a fashionable cynic, venting a shallow disappointment with men and things in well-turned homilies upon the way of the world. Playing up to his man the fool rails on Lady Fortune in good set terms. The philosopher is hooked and the fool lands his fish with a solemn descant upon the passage of time. Jaques, completely taken in, marvels that a fool should be so *deep-contemplative*.

We would give a good deal to have been present at this meeting, but Shakespeare decided otherwise and for a very good reason. If we had actually *seen* Jaques so obviously mocked, crowing like chanticleer but missing the whole point of the jest, we could never for a moment have regarded him as anything else but a figure of fun. But by merely *reporting* the incident Shakespeare leaves us to draw our own conclusions. He is not unwilling that Jaques should up to a point impose on his audience and be for the purposes of the play accepted at his own valuation. This melancholy gentleman was a popular stage character and none knew better than Shakespeare that a dash of sentimental cynicism goes down very well in a light comedy. Jaques is to be its purveyor and he must not therefore be too plainly exposed as a counterfeit philosopher who does not even know when the laugh is against him. Again our dramatist means to have it both ways. He will entertain us on the lower level with Jaques as a moralist and let those who like him thus be taken in if they will. But those who look a little deeper shall also have their fun.

Shakespeare so artfully plays this double game that it is quite possible to enjoy the comedy without allowing ourselves to become aware that the melancholy Jaques is, first to last, a purely comic character. Some critics have even gone so far as to compare him with Hamlet and most actors deliver his speech on the seven ages of man to a hushed audience as though it were a deep epitome of human experience.

G. K. HUNTER

Twelfth Night

A READING OF *As You Like It* together with *Twelfth Night* will soon
reveal that the two plays are by the same hand. Both centre on the
vision of happiness through love, as it is seen by a highly-born heroine
who is condemned to serve out her love in a strange country, disguised
as a boy. Both plays set the loving self-awareness of this heroine against
a gallery of poseurs, lamed by self-love (and the consequent lack of
self-awareness), and show her depth of sanity in her capacity to play
the strange role that the harsh world sets her, with efficiency but without losing faith in the true identity to which fate and her own efforts
will eventually return her. Both plays contain important "wise-fool"
roles, in which the fool (Touchstone or Feste) is largely detached from
the loving and self-loving world, knowing better than most the inevitability of self-deception, but less than at least one (the heroine) the value
of implication in the Human Dilemma.

The likeness of the two plays is considerable, but it appears in the
mechanics rather than the effects. The two professional fools may
indeed serve to focus the differences as well as the similarities. A. C.
Bradley remarked of Feste that "he would never have dreamed of
marrying Audrey." Critics today are properly chary about the kind of
criticism which tries to fit characters out of one play into another ("we
can imagine the difference at Elsinore if only Hamlet could have been
married to Lady Macbeth") but in this case the remark seems to com-
press conveniently an important difference between the two plays. Feste
(unlike Touchstone) has no history, and this affects his function in the
play. I have already quoted Touchstone's use of his own experience,
past and present, of Jane Smile in the past and Audrey in the present,
to make points about love and pastoralism. Feste has no personal life to
use as a "stalking-horse"; there is no self-parody in his statements; his
gaze is fixed relentlessly on the temperaments and actions of others,

Reprinted by permission of the author from *Shakespeare: The Later Comedies*. Published
for the British Council and the National Book League by Longmans, Green, and Co. Ltd. First
printed 1962; reprinted with additions to bibliography, 1964.

with a clear eye for their foibles and weaknesses, for the self-indulgent melancholia of Orsino:

> the tailor make thy doublet of changeable taffeta, for thy mind is a very opal,
> (II. iv. 72–73)

for the wilful grieving of Olivia:

> the more fool [you] Madonna, to mourn for your brother's soul, being in heaven,   (I. v. 65–66)

for the self-love (and so self-ignorance) of Malvolio:

> I say there is no darkness but ignorance, in which thou art more puzzled than the Egyptians in their fog.   (IV. ii. 41–43)

It is typical of Feste's role as the detached onlooker that we are uncertain if he was ever fully involved in the plot against Malvolio. Certainly he was willing to appear as the "wise" Sir Topas ministering to the "fool" Malvolio, for that demonstrated neatly how "the whirligig of time brings in his revenges," but the involvement seems limited to this intellectual kind of pleasure in consequences. Feste is not to be circumscribed by the subplot grouping of Sir Toby, Maria, Sir Andrew, nor can he be supposed to share their "eat, drink and be merry" philosophy, except as it suits his purpose. He is the onlooker who judges but is never judged; in this way he is bound to be much nearer to the centre of the play than is Touchstone.

The changed and more central role of the fool in this play is symptomatic of a change of focus in the whole design. No longer is affectation or self-indulgence a weakness which can be put aside blandly, as it is by Rosalind. In *As You Like It* Phebe and Jaques can be put in their places, in a dance of living and loving, by self-control and self-awareness, but without self-sacrifice. In *Twelfth Night,* affectation is everywhere — among the heroic as among the foolish, among the central characters as among the marginal — and self-sacrifice is necessarily involved if it is to be defeated. Rosalind is able to use her disguise as a genuine and joyous extension of her personality; Viola suffers constriction and discomfiture in *her* role. It is properly representative that the most famous speeches by the disguised Rosalind are her teasing comments on Orlando, such as that at IV.i. 83 ff.:

> The poor world is almost six thousand years old, and in all this time there was not any man died in his own person, videlicet, in a love-cause . . . men have died from time to time, and worms have eaten them, but not for love.

while the most famous speech of the disguised Viola is the melancholy description of her own imagined fate:

> She never told her love,
> But let concealment, like a worm i' th' bud,
> Feed on her damask cheek. She pin'd in thought;
> And with a green and yellow melancholy
> She sat like Patience on a monument
> Smiling at grief. Was not this love indeed?   (II. iv. 109–14)

— further constricted, as the speech is, in the context of Orsino's assumption that women cannot love.

The vision of happiness is thus for Viola a smiling through tears, a vision all the more poignant for its unlikeliness to be fulfilled. To say this is to make Viola sound like the archetype for much modern "brave little woman" sentimentality. And she is not: the play is too busy to let her even seem so. The sentiment is placed in a current of cross-intrigues which keeps it from the stagnation of sentimentality. Happiness is a perpetual possibility which has to be shelved away as soon as it is exposed (for matters, not hostile, but more immediately pressing, always intervene); it is a single thread in a broadloom that is largely made up of threats and deceptions. It is one of the functions of the large-scale and fully developed subplot of this play to complicate each of the visits that Viola makes to the house of Olivia, and to cross-hatch the final comedy of errors between Sebastian and Viola.

But the complications introduced by the sub-plot are not to be limited to the intrigues it contains; what we have here is not a simple world of below-stairs bumbling and aping (as in *Much Ado*) but a real, even if easily deflected, threat to the security of princely natures and developed sensibilities. On the self-indulgence of Olivia and Orsino must be laid at least some of the blame for the presumptuousness of Malvolio and the idle mischief of Sir Toby. Malvolio's aspiration to join the aristocracy is not absurd; his disguise in smiles and yellow stockings can be seen as a nastier variant of the "mental disguise" of Orsino and Olivia — their willingness to act on temporary obsessions, and to forget the continuity of their lives. All are presented as victims of a need to hide from the isolated truth (and here Viola, though her disguise is forced on her and not chosen, must be joined with the others): Olivia cannot bear to be known for what she is — a healthy and nubile woman; Viola cannot permit herself to be known for what she is — a girl; Orsino cannot bear to be known for what he is — a lover in love with the idea of love; Sir Toby cannot bear to be known for a parasite, Sir Andrew for a fool, Malvolio for a steward. The process of the play is one which allows these truths to be bearable (or socially organized) at the end of the action, not by developing characters to a greater understanding, but simply by moving the plot around till the major characters each find themselves opposite a desirable partner and an escape hatch from absurdity. The new pattern at the end is seen not only as personally satisfying, but also as socially desirable, certain pretenders to civility (notably Malvolio and Sir Andrew) being rejected from the pattern (as in Restoration Comedy), in which the others express their own superior natures. It is true that there is a degree of "Jonsonian" social realism in the play's image of an effete aristocracy threatened by a determined upstart; the economic basis of the relationship between Sir Toby and Sir Andrew is clearly stated (II.iv. 170 ff.), and the marriage of Sir Toby and Maria is more a piece of social justice than a contribution to any final dance of reconciliation. But this dance itself is not to be explained in social terms; the principal emotion involved in the denouement is the sense of release from the complexity and isolation of outer disguise or inner obsession; and this is a personal and individual matter, to which society is merely accessory:

> When . . . golden time convents,
> A solemn combination shall be made
> Of our dear souls. Meantime, sweet sister,
> We will not part from hence. Cesario, come;
> For so you shall be, while you are a man;
> But when in other habits you are seen,
> Orsino's mistress, and his fancy's queen. (V. i. 368–74)

But we may well feel that the play has related the dream world of "golden time" too securely to the class struggle around it to allow this to be more than a partial reconciliation. The amount of space that the denouement gives to Malvolio (about one hundred lines out of a total of one hundred and seventy-five) may seem to be indicative of Shakespeare's waning interest in these glamorous aristocrats. In *As You Like It* the dance of lovers was broken by the solitary Jaques but was not marred by him, for he too had found a milieu in which he could be himself:

> [*to Duke*] You to your former honour I bequeath;
> Your patience and your virtue well deserves it.
> [*to Orlando*] You to a love that your true faith doth merit;
> . . .   So, to your pleasures:
> I am for other than for dancing measures. (V. iv. 180–7)

But the exit of Malvolio:

> I'll be revenged on the whole pack of you (V. i. 364)

is more difficult to fit in. The Duke instructs servants to

>   Pursue him, and entreat him to a peace,

but we are hardly convinced that this will be effective. The happiness of the lovers would seem to have been bought at a price which excludes Malvolio, and we may feel that this circumscribes and diminishes the final effect of their happiness.

It is another function of the subplot in *Twelfth Night* to complement the lyric world of the high-born characters with a robust and self-sufficient grossness so that a more complete image of society emerges. I have already suggested that the combination of wit and sentiment serves, in both *Much Ado* and *As You Like It,* to keep the comedy from extremes of either harshness or pulpiness. *Twelfth Night* is not, however, a comedy of wit. It is, on the other hand, the most poetical (and musical) of the comedies; this is not to say that a higher proportion of the lines are poetry, but that it is more shot through and through by the lyric abandon of poetic utterance:

>   VIOLA: If I did love you in my master's flame,
>   With such a suff'ring, such a deadly life,
>   In your denial I would find no sense;
>   I would not understand it.
>   OLIVIA: Why, what would you?
>   VIOLA: Make me a willow cabin at your gate,
>   And call upon my soul within the house;
>   Write loyal cantons of contemned love
>   And sing them loud even in the dead of night;
>   Halloo your name to the reverberate hills,
>   And make the babbling gossip of the air
>   Cry out 'Olivia!' O, you should not rest
>   Between the elements of air and earth
>   But you should pity me.   (I. v. 248–60)

Poetic abandon of this kind is required in *Twelfth Night,* because there is so little that the characters, disguised, obsessed and frustrated as they are, can do; they are obliged to live out their potentialities rather than deeds — potentialities (here as in the "she never told her love" speech) dramatically enlarged in the mirror of a nostalgia for the impossible. This powerfully affects the image of the lover that the play gives us. In *As You Like It* we met the absurdity of the lover in Orlando's verses; but the verse is only a by-product of the loving personality. In Orsino, on the other hand, as in Olivia, the poetic abandon of love is given its bent and allowed a full range of languorous evocation:

> If music be the food of love, play on,
> Give me excess of it, that, surfeiting,
> The appetite may sicken and so die.
> That strain again! It had a dying fall;
> O, it came o'er my ear like the sweet sound
> That breathes upon a bank of violets,
> Stealing and giving odour! Enough, no more;
> 'Tis not so sweet now as it was before.   (I. i. 1–8)

The situation is somewhat similar to that of Silvius and Phebe in *As You Like It*, high poetical but illusory; this time, however, because it stands at the centre of the play, it cannot be shot down by wit; Orsino and Olivia are too powerful to be scored against and pushed aside. Both indeed are, as has been remarked, "unlikely candidates for affectation"; Orsino is categorically stated, in the exposition, to be

> A noble duke, in nature as in name.   (I. ii. 25)

and Olivia, in her rule of her household and her distinction between Feste and Malvolio, shows a rare poise, even in the midst of her excess:

> O, you are sick of self-love, Malvolio, and taste with a distemper'd appetite. To be generous, guiltless, and of free disposition, is to take those things for bird-bolts that you deem cannon bullets. There is no slander in an allow'd fool, though he do nothing but rail; nor no railing in a known discreet man, though he do nothing but reprove.   (I. v. 85–90)

If such people are deluded, then their poetical delusions must be *self*-cured; it is for this reason, I suppose, that the play offers, beside *their* worlds, other worlds of experience which they can react to and discover, and discovering, evaluate properly (because of their fundamental nobility); with this evidence we judge them on their potential insight, seen against the others' incurable blindness. That love is both absurd and ennobling is a point that all these comedies have made; here in a world where all are disguised or deluded we need the grosser loves (and delusions) of Andrew, Toby and Malvolio, whose sensuality is an important element in his character, to give a scale to the high poetical delusions of Orsino and Olivia. A glance at a long and complex scene, like Act III, scene iv, may indicate how this is achieved. The scene opens with the comic incoherence of an Olivia plagued by love — very similar to the comedy of Rosalind already quoted (II.ii. 204–9) — but it moves immediately to the related love-madness of Malvolio, the relevance of this being stated categorically:

> OLIVIA: Go call him hither. I am mad as he,
> If sad and merry madness equal be.   (III. iv. 14–15)

Malvolio's lunatic power to find encouragement in insults reflects directly on Olivia's refusal to accept Viola's words, but it also highlights the self-knowledge she shows in the face of her own madness; for he flies straight into a state where he is the very puppet of his own obsession, incapable of human conversation:

> MALVOLIO: Go, hang yourselves all! you are idle shallow things: I am not
> of your element: you shall know more hereafter.   [*Exit.*
> SIR TOBY: Is't possible?
> FAB.: If this were play'd upon a stage now, I could condemn it as an
> improbable fiction.
> SIR TOBY: His very genius hath taken the infection of the device, man.
> (III. iv. 117–24)

The next episode contrasts the cowardice of Viola with that of Sir Andrew, and again the contrast is handled as one between laughing at the person and laughing at the situation. Andrew is sublimely ignorant of the difference between noble and ignoble behaviour:

> Plague on't; an I thought he had been valiant, and so cunning in fence, I'd
> have seen him damn'd ere I'd have challeng'd him. Let him let the matter
> slip, and I'll give him my horse, grey Capilet.   (III. iv. 270–3)

To Fabian and Sir Toby the comedy of the cowardly Cesario is no different from that of the cowardly Sir Andrew:

> SIR TOBY: I have his horse to take up the quarrel: I have persuaded him
> the youth's a devil.
> FABIAN: He is as horribly conceited of him; and pants and looks pale, as if
> a bear were at his heels,   (III. iv. 277–80)

but we react differently. Viola directs our attention to her inner dilemma:

> Pray God defend me! A little thing would make me tell them how much I
> lack of a man.   (III. iv. 286–7)

and so (while we laugh) we share her view of the situation; the gross level of the practical joke that Fabian and Sir Toby are conducting is being judged by Viola's reaction to it no less than she is being judged by their contrived situation.

In among these pranks Shakespeare places two passages of high-bred sensibility. Olivia and Viola meet briefly (for seventeen lines) and reveal their natures:

> OLIVIA: I have said too much unto a heart of stone,
>   And laid mine honour too unchary out:
>   There's something in me that reproves my fault;
>   But such a headstrong potent fault it is,
>   That it but mocks reproof.
> VIOLA: With the same 'haviour that your passion bears
>   Goes on my master's griefs.   (III. iv. 191–7)

In the context of the fake conflict of Sir Andrew's challenge, this real conflict of sensibilities and self-awareness make an immediate effect of noble honesty; it is not the self-indulgence that we note so much as the effort to deal with emotion. A second and more extended expression of the emotional world of noble persons comes at the end of the scene. Sir Toby's plan to trap Viola in her cowardice is turned back on his own head (quite literally) by the intervention of Antonio; but the farce turns towards tragedy in the arrest and apparent betrayal of Antonio.

Shakespeare's handling of this is extremely complex: the natural release by a just revenge on the bullies is suspended; they are left plotting new torments for Viola, while Antonio is haled away to prison; but the centre of the episode is in none of these, but in the sudden and rapturous vision that the refined sensibility will not always have to endure the context of disguise and discomfiture:

> VIOLA: He nam'd Sebastian: I my brother know
>   Yet living in my glass; even such and so
>   In favour was my brother; and he went
>   Still in this fashion, colour, ornament,
>   For him I imitate: O, if it prove,
>   Tempests are kind, and salt waves fresh in love!
>   (III. iv. 363–8)

Beside this vision of escape and reconciliation, the difficulties of denouement fall away, and the threat from the bullies, still crouching in the corner, suddenly seems absurd and unimportant; for the constructive powers of noble minds are not within their scope, and this has been given witness to, once again, even in the face of Antonio's betrayal:

> I hate ingratitude more in a man
> Than lying, vainness, babbling drunkenness,
> Or any taint of vice whose strong corruption
> Inhabits our frail blood.   (III. iv. 338–41)

But the reconciliation is an *escape* here, not a conquest, as in *As You Like It*. The final dance of reconciliation is bound to seem circumscribed, for the role of Chance (which brings Sebastian to Illyria) is (unlike that of Hymen) that of the master and not servant to the heroine:

> What will become of this? As I am man,
> My state is desperate for my master's love;
> As I am woman — now alas the day! —
> What thriftless sights shall poor Olivia breathe!
> O time! thou must untangle this, not I;
> It is too hard a knot for me t'untie.   (II. ii. 34–39)

The play ends with a nonsense-song which earlier critics thought was plain nonsense and therefore spurious, but which modern critics usually see as an extended comment on the central ideas of the play:

> When that I was and a little tiny boy,
> > With hey, ho, the wind and the rain,
> A foolish thing was but a toy,
> > For the rain it raineth every day.

> But when I came to man's estate, etc.
> 'Gainst knaves and thieves men shut their gate, etc.

> But when I came, alas! to wive, etc.
> By swaggering could I never thrive, etc.

> But when I came unto my beds, etc.
> With toss-pots still had drunken heads, etc.

> A great while ago the world began, etc.
> But that's all one, our play is done,
> > And we'll strive to please you every day.

Very little is clear in this; maturing seems to be looked at as a process in which folly loses its status, though most things stay the same ("the rain it raineth every day"), and have stayed the same since the world began. The song ends with a deliberate refusal to philosophize even this far, however: "don't look for causal connections; a play is a play and not a treatise." In its illogicality and its bittersweet sense of the need to submit to illogicality, the song is a fitting conclusion to the play in which happiness itself is seen as illogical and chancy. The very name of the play should suggest the same mood to us. "Twelfth night" is often taken as meaning simply "revelry," but though it is still in the season of Misrule, twelfth night is at the very limit of the season:

Hedge crickets sing; and now with treble soft
The red-breast whistles from a garden-croft;
And gathering swallows twitter in the skies.

Seen in the context of Shakespeare's *oeuvre,* this melancholy mood of comedy in *Twelfth Night* cannot well be kept apart from the tragic vision of the plays like *Troilus and Cressida* and *Hamlet* which are its contemporaries. The comedy ends with happiness for some, but the happiness has no inevitability, and the final song sounds perilously like a tune whistled through the surrounding darkness. The fate of Malvolio is proper enough in the context of revelry, but the context is hardly strong enough to drown completely the overtones of *Hamlet;* the malcontented outsider is not *always* despicable. In *Twelfth Night* the impetus towards reconciliation is sufficiently tentative to allow such thoughts, and in such thoughts lies the death of Comedy.

L. G. SALINGAR

The Design of Twelfth Night and Its Sources

SHAKESPEARE's intentions may stand out more clearly when one compares his treatment of the Viola story with its possible or probable sources. The ultimate source is held to be the anonymous Sienese comedy, *Gl'Ingannati* (*The Deceived*), first performed at a carnival of 1531 and frequently reprinted, translated, or imitated in the course of the sixteenth century. Shakespeare may also have known Bandello's story, which follows the plot of *Gl'Ingannati* closely, omitting the subordinate comic parts; and he probably knew Riche's *Apolonius and Silla* (1581), derived indirectly and with variations from Bandello. Another source of the main plot must have been the *Menaechmi* of Plautus, which presumably had already contributed something to *Gl'Ingannati*, but affects the composition of *Twelfth Night* more directly by way of *The Comedy of Errors*. In any case, Shakespeare's situations were part of the common stock of classical and medieval romance, as Manningham saw at one of the first performances of *Twelfth Night*, when he noted in his diary that it was "much like the Commedy of Errores, or Menechmi in Plautus, but most like and neere to that in Italian called *Inganni*" (one of the off-shoots of *Gl'Ingannati*).

There are four essential characters common to *Gl'Ingannati*, Bandello, Riche, and Shakespeare; namely, a lover, a heroine in his service disguised as a page, her twin brother (who at first has disappeared), and a second heroine. The basic elements common to all four plots are: the heroine's secret love for her master; her employment as go-between, leading to the complication of a cross-wooing; and a final solution by means of the unforeseen arrival of the missing twin.

If Shakespeare knew Bandello or *Gl'Ingannati*, he altered their material radically. The Italians both take the romance motif of a heroine's

From the *Shakespeare Quarterly*, IX (1958), pp. 120–8. This section of a longer essay, "The Design of Twelfth Night," has been reprinted with permission of the author and the *Shakespeare Quarterly*, who have also given permission for the omission of original footnotes. Footnote 1 was written for this edition by the author. Title provided by the present editor.

constancy and love-service, set it in a realistic bourgeois environment, and rationalize it with respectful irony. In Bandello, the irony is severely rational — because it is a tale of love, "the wonder ceases at once." In *Gl'Ingannati,* the tone is whimsical. "Two lessons above all you will extract from this play," says the Prologue: "how much chance and good fortune can do in matters of love; and how much long patience is worth in such cases, accompanied by good advice." Both Italian authors give the heroine a strong motive for assuming her disguise, in that the lover has previously returned her affection, but has now forgotten her and turned elsewhere. Both provide her with a formidable father in the background and a foster-mother like Juliet's Nurse, who admonishes and helps her; and both credit her with the intention of bilking her rival if she can. On the other side, they both respect the code of courtly love to the extent of stressing the lover's penitence at the end, and his recognition that he must repay the heroine for her devotion. "I believe," he says in the play, "that this is certainly the will of God, who must have taken pity on this virtuous maiden and on my soul, that it should not go to perdition. . . ."

Riche keeps this framework of sentiment, vulgarizes the narrative, and changes some of the material circumstances, generally in the direction of an Arcadian romance.

Shakespeare, for his part, changes the story fundamentally, broadening the interest and at the same time making the whole situation more romantically improbable, more melancholy at some points, more fantastic at others. He stiffens the heroine's loyalty, but deprives her of her original motive, her initiative, and her family. In place of these, he gives her the background of a vague "Messaline" and a romantic shipwreck, for which he may have taken a hint, but no more, from the episode of the shipwreck in Riche. Shakespeare's Viola, then, is a more romantic heroine than the rest, and the only one to fall in love after assuming her disguise. At the same time, however, Shakespeare enlarges the role of her twin brother and gives unprecedented weight to coincidence in the dénouement, which in both Italian stories is brought about more rationally, by the deliberate action of the heroine and her nurse; so that Shakespeare's Viola is also unique in that her happiness is due to "good fortune" more than "long patience," and to "good advice" not at all.

In his exposition, therefore, Shakespeare sketches a situation from romance in place of a logical intrigue. But the purpose, or at any rate, the effect, of his plan is to shift attention at the outset from the circumstances of the love story to the sentiments as such, especially in their more mysterious and irrational aspects. Shakespeare may have taken hints, for Orsino and Olivia, from his predecessors' comments on the "error" of "following them that fly from us." But however that may be, his comedy now consists in the triumph of natural love over affectation and melancholy. And, taken together, the leading characters in *Twelfth Night* form the most subtle portrayal of the psychology of love that Shakespeare had yet drawn.

Viola's love is fresh and direct, and gathers strength as the play advances. When she first appears, Viola mourns her brother, like Olivia, and by choice would join Olivia in her seclusion:

> O, that I serv'd that lady,
> And might not be deliver'd to the world,
> Till I had made mine own occasion mellow,
> What my estate is.   (I. ii. 40)

Shakespeare makes the most here of the vagueness surrounding Viola; she seems the child of the sea, and of time. But even when her feelings and her problem have become distinct she still commits herself to "time" with a gentle air of detachment:

> What will become of this? As I am a man,
> My state is desperate for my master's love;
> As I am a woman, — now alas the day! —
> What thriftless sighs shall poor Olivia breathe!
> O time, thou must untangle this, not I,
> It is too hard a knot for me t'untie.   (II. ii. 37)

She has none of the vehement determination of the Italian heroines, and, though nimble-witted, she is less resourceful and high-spirited than Rosalind. She foreshadows Perdita and Miranda in the romantically adolescent quality of her part.

There are stronger colors than this in Viola, admittedly. Before she appears on the stage, Orsino has spoken of the capacity for love inherent in a woman's devoted sorrow for her brother; and in two scenes in the middle of the play Viola herself speaks in more passionate terms. But in both cases her own feeling seems muffled or distorted, since she is acting a part, and in both cases her tone is distinctly theatrical. She tells Olivia how, if she were Orsino, she would

> Write loyal cantons of contemned love,
> And sing them loud even in the dead of night;
> Holla your name to the reverberate hills,
> And make the babbling gossip of the air
> Cry out 'Olivia!';   (I.v.279)

she tells Orsino, on the other hand, that her imaginary sister

> never told her love,
> But let concealment, like a worm i'the bud
> Feed on her damask cheek; —   (II.iv.111)

— in each case, with an overtone of romantic excess. She does not speak out in her own voice, therefore, until the later scenes, when the more vigorous (and more artificial) emotions of the older pair have had full play. Meanwhile, the hints of excess in her two fictitious declarations of love reflect on the others as well as herself: she speaks for Orsino in the spirit of his injunction to "be clamorous, and leap all civil bounds"; while her image of repressed desire could apply to Olivia. Her own development in the comedy is closely attuned to the others'.

Shakespeare begins the play with Orsino. He follows Riche in making the lover in his comedy a duke (not, as with the Italians, a citizen), who has been a warrior but has now "become a scholar in love's school." Orsino suffers from the melancholy proper to courtly and "heroical" love; and Shakespeare fixes attention on his passion, which is more violent and "fantastical" than in the other versions of the story, by keeping Orsino inactive in his court to dramatize his own feelings like Richard II. Unlike the Italian lovers, he has not been fickle, yet changefulness is the very essence of his condition. He twice calls for music in the play, but there is no harmony in himself. Within a few lines, he countermands the first order, to apostrophize the spirit of love:

> Enough, no more!
> 'Tis not so sweet now as it was before.
> O spirit of love, how quick and fresh art thou,
> That, notwithstanding thy capacity
> Receiveth as the sea, nought enters there,
> Of what validity and pitch soe'er,
> But falls into abatement and low price,
> Even in a minute: so full of shapes is fancy
> That it alone is high fantastical.   (I.i.7)

This apostrophe carries opposing meanings. "Quick" and "fresh," coming after "sicken" a few lines before, imply the vigor of life, but they also prolong the grosser sense of "appetite" and "surfeiting." The sea image glorifies Orsino's "spirit of love" and, in relation to the drama as a whole, it prepares the way for the sea-change that comes to Viola and Sebastian; but it also leads on to the image of Sir Toby "drowned" in drink (I. v. 135). And Orsino's most striking metaphors here, those of sinking and "low price," suggest that what the speaker largely feels is chill and dismay. Nothing has any value by comparison with love; but also, nothing has any lasting, intrinsic value for a lover. Later, referring to the sea-fight, Orsino utters a similar paradox when he describes the "fame and honour" Antonio had won in "a bawbling vessel . . . For shallow draught and bulk unprizable" (V.i.52). But there, the paradox enhances Antonio's courage; here, it is depressing. For Orsino, the only constant feature of love is instability. He tells Viola (II.iv.17) that all true lovers are

> Unstaid and skittish in all motions else
> Save in the constant image of the creature
> That is beloved;

a moment later, it is the "image" that changes —

> For, boy, however we do praise ourselves,
> Our fancies are more giddy and unfirm,
> More longing, wavering, sooner lost and worn
> Than women's are; —

and then, as he thinks of Olivia, it is the woman's "appetite," not the man's, that can "suffer surfeit, cloyment, and revolt" (II.iv.98). Feste sketches the life of such a lover with fitting ambiguity: "I would have men of such constancy put to sea, that their business might be every thing and their intent every where; for that's it that always makes a good voyage of nothing" (II.iv.75); they dissipate their advantages and can be satisfied with illusions. By its very nature, then, Orsino's love for Olivia is self-destructive, subject to time and change. Although, or rather, because, it is "all as hungry as the sea," it is impossible to satisfy. And it seems almost without an object, or incommensurate with any object, a "monstrosity" in the same sense as Troilus' love for Cressida, in its grasping after the infinite.

Moreover, Orsino's "spirit of love" seems something outside the rest of his personality, a tyrant from whom he longs to escape. His desires pursue him "like fell and cruel hounds." He wants music to diminish his passion, to relieve it with the thought of death. And when at last he confronts Olivia, something like hatred bursts through his conventional phrases of love-homage: "yond same sovereign cruelty" (II.iv) is now (V.i.) a "perverse," "uncivil lady," "ingrate and unauspicious," "the marble-breasted tyrant." In his jealous rage he feels himself "at point of death":

> Why should I not, had I the heart to do it,
> Like to the Egyptian thief at point of death,
> Kill what I love? a savage jealousy
> That sometime savours nobly.   (V. i. 115)

In all this, however, there is as much injured vanity as anything else. His "fancy" is at the point of dying, not his heart; and it is fully consistent with his character that he can swerve almost at once to Viola, gratified and relieved by the surprise of her identity and the full disclosure of her devotion to himself. His emotions, then, give a powerful upsurge to the play, but they are kept within the bounds of comedy. His real "error," in Shakespeare, is that he only imagines himself to be pursuing love. Olivia's, correspondingly, is that she only imagines herself to be flying from it.

With Olivia, even more than with Orsino, Shakespeare diverges from his possible sources, making her a much more prominent and interesting character than her prototypes. In the Italian stories, the second heroine is heiress to a wealthy old dotard, is kept out of sight most of the time, and is treated with ribald irony for her amorous forwardness. In *Apolonius and Silla*, she is a wealthy widow. In all three, she is considered only as rival and pendant to the Viola-heroine. Shakespeare, however, makes her a virgin, psychologically an elder sister to Viola, and better able to sustain the comedy of awakening desire. At the same time, she is the mistress of a noble household, and hence the focus of the sub-plot as well as the main plot. When she first appears, she can rebuke Malvolio with aristocratic courtesy (I.v.94): "To be generous, guiltless, and of free disposition, is to take those things for bird-bolts that you deem cannon-bullets." But Olivia, like Orsino — like Malvolio, even — suffers from ignorance of herself, and must be cured of affectation; as Sebastian says (V.i. 262), "nature to her bias drew in that."

Her vow of mourning has a tinge of the same aristocratic extravagance as Orsino's "spirit of love." Orsino compares her to an angry Diana; but then there follows at once the account of her vow, which already begins to disclose the comic, unseasonable side of her assumed coldness:

> The element itself, till seven years' heat,
> Shall not behold her face at ample view;
> But, like a cloistress, she will veiled walk,
> And water once a day her chamber round
> With eye-offending brine: all this to season
> A brother's dead love, which she would keep fresh
> And lasting in her sad remembrance.   (I.i.25)

Olivia is to be rescued from her cloister (like Diana's priestess in *The Comedy of Errors* or Hermia in *A Midsummer Night's Dream*) and exposed to the sunshine. Feste warns her, in gentle mockery, that she is a "fool"; the hood does not make the monk, and "as there is no true cuckold but calamity, so beauty's a flower" (I.v.) She is obliged to unveil her beauty, and has natural vanity enough to claim that " 'twill endure wind and weather" (I.v.246); and Viola's speech, which stirs her heart, is also a form of comic retribution, hollaing her name to "the reverberate hills" and "the babling gossip of the air"—

> O, you should not rest
> Between the elements of air and earth,
> But you should pity me. (I.v.281)

"Element" is made one of the comic catchwords of the play.

The comic reversal of Olivia's attitude culminates in her declaration of love to Viola, the most delicate and yet impressive speech in the play (III.i.150). It is now Olivia's turn to plead against "scorn," to "unclasp the book of her secret soul" to Viola — and, equally, to herself. After two lines, she turns to the same verse form of impersonal, or extra-personal, "sentences" in rhyme that Shakespeare gives to other heroines at their moment of truth:

> O, what a deal of scorn looks beautiful
> In the contempt and anger of his lip!
> A murd'rous guilt shows not itself more soon
> Than love that would seem hid: love's night is noon.
> Cesario, by the roses of the spring,
> By maidhood, honour, truth, and every thing,
> I love thee so, that, maugre all thy pride,
> Nor wit nor reason can my passion hide.
> Do not extort thy reasons from this clause,
> For that I woo, thou therefore hast no cause;
> But rather reason thus with reason fetter,
> Love sought is good, but given unsought is better.

Having already thrown off her original veil, Olivia now breaks through the concealments of her pride, her modesty, and her feminine "wit." Her speech is mainly a vehement persuasion to love, urged "by the roses of the spring." Yet she keeps her dignity, and keeps it all the more in view of the secondary meaning latent in her words, her timid fear that Cesario's scorn is not the disdain of rejection at all but the scorn of conquest. Logically, indeed, her first rhyming couplet implies just this, implies that his cruel looks are the signs of a guilty lust rising to the surface; and this implication is carried on as she speaks of his "pride" (with its hint of sexual desire), and into her last lines, with their covert pleading not to "extort" a callous advantage from her confession. But in either case — whatever Cesario's intentions — love now appears to Olivia as a startling paradox: guilty, even murderous, an irruption of misrule; and at the same time irrepressible, fettering reason, and creating its own light out of darkness. And, in either case, the conclusion to her perplexities is a plain one — "Love sought is good, but given un-sought is better." This is Shakespeare's departure from the moral argu-ment of his predecessors, and it marks the turning-point of *Twelfth Night*.

There is still a trace of irony attaching to Olivia, in that her wooing is addressed to another woman and has been parodied beforehand in Maria's forged love-letter (II.v). And this irony pursues her to the end, even in her marriage, when once again she tries, and fails, "To keep in darkness what occasion now Reveals before 'tis ripe" (V.i.151). But from the point of her declaration to Viola, the way is clear for the reso-lution of the whole comedy on the plane of sentiment. In terms of senti-ment, she has justified her gift of love to a stranger. She is soon completely sure of herself, and in the later scenes she handles Sir Toby, Orsino, and Cesario-Sebastian with brusque decision; while her demon of austerity is cast out through Malvolio. The main action of *Twelfth Night*, then, is planned with a suggestive likeness to a revel, in which Olivia is masked, Orsino's part is "giddy" and "fantastical," Viola-Sebastian is the mysterious stranger — less of a character and more of a poetic symbol than the others — and in the end, as Feste says of his own "interlude" with Malvolio, "the whirligig of time brings in his revenges."

Although Olivia's declaration forms the crisis of the main action, the resolution of the plot has still to be worked out. And here Shakespeare departs in a new way from his predecessors. Shakespeare's Sebastian, by character and adventures, has little in common with the brother in *Gl'Ingannati*, and still less with Silla's brother in Riche; but nearly every-thing in common — as Manningham presumably noticed — with the visiting brother in Plautus, Menaechmus of Syracuse. And Antonio's part in the plot (though not his character) is largely that of Menaech-mus' slave in Plautus, while his emotional role stems from the Aegeon story that Shakespeare himself had already added to *Menaechmi* in *The Comedy of Errors*. These Plautine elements in the brother's story have been altered in *Gl'Ingannati* and dropped from, or camouflaged in, *Apolonius and Silla*. Whichever of the latter Shakespeare used for Viola, therefore, he deliberately reverted to Plautus for Sebastian, sometimes drawing on his own elaborations in *The Comedy of Errors*, but mainly going back directly to the original.[1]

1 The article in *Shakespeare Quarterly* shows at length that, as Manningham seems to have noticed in 1602, Sebastian's adventures closely resemble those of the hero of Plautus's *Menaechmi*, a play well known in the sixteenth century. A confirmatory detail is Sebastian's reference to "Messaline" in II.i. There is no such town as "Messaline," but the name is almost certainly derived from the line in *Menaechmi* II.i where the hero's companion says that in their search for his lost twin they have visited "every section the sea washes" — "Istrians, Spaniards, *Massilians, Illyrians* (*Massiliensis, Hilurios*)." Presumably Shakespeare's memory linked *Massilia* (*Marseilles*) and *Illyria* together. In classical times, the scene of Plautus's comedy, Epidamnus (now Durazzo), was part of the province of Illyria — which becomes the setting of Shakespeare's comedy.

Hence the second half of *Twelfth Night* is largely more farcical than its predecessors, whereas the first half had been, in a sense, more romantic. Shakespeare thus provides a telling finale, proper, as Dr. Johnson observes, to the stage. But he does much more than this. His farcical dénouement gives tangible shape to the notion of misrule inherent in his romantic exposition. Faults of judgment in the first part of *Twelfth Night* are answered with mistakes of identity in the second, while the action swirls to a joyful ending through a crescendo of errors. And by the same manoeuvre, Shakespeare charges his romance with a new emotional significance, bringing it nearer to tragedy.

How are Viola and Olivia to be freed? In *Apolonius and Silla,* the widow, pregnant after her welcome to Silla's brother, demands justice of the disguised heroine, thus forcing her to reveal herself and clearing the way for her marriage to the duke. Only when the rumor of this wedding has spread abroad does the wandering brother return to the scene and espouse the widow. In the Italian stories, the heroine reaches an understanding with her master by her own devices and the aid of her nurse, without any kind of help from the arrival of her brother; and this is a logical solution, since the heroine's love-service is the clear center of interest. But Shakespeare has been more broadly concerned with love as a force in life as a whole. He has shifted the emphasis to the two older lovers, keeping Viola's share of passion in reserve. And even after the crisis, he continues to withhold the initiative the Italians had given her. Shakespeare is alone in making the heroine reveal herself *after her* brother's marriage with the second heroine, as a consequence of it. And the whole Plautine sequence in *Twelfth Night* is designed to lead to this conclusion. Hence, while the first half of Shakespeare's comedy dwells in self-deception in love, the second half stresses the benevolent irony of fate.

JOSEPH H. SUMMERS

The Masks of Twelfth Night

LOVE AND its fulfillment are primary in Shakespeare's comedies. Its conflicts are often presented in terms of the battle of the generations. At the beginning of the plays the bliss of the young lovers is usually barred by an older generation of parents and rulers, a group which has supposedly experienced its own fulfillment in the past and which is now concerned with preserving old forms or fulfilling new ambitions. The comedies usually end with the triumph of young love, a triumph in which the lovers make peace with their elders and themselves assume adulthood and often power. The revolutionary force of love becomes an added element of vitality in a re-established society.

Twelfth Night does not follow the customary pattern. In this play the responsible older generation has been abolished, and there are no parents at all. In the first act we are rapidly introduced into a world in which the ruler is a love-sick Duke — in which young ladies, fatherless and motherless, embark on disguised actions, or rule, after a fashion, their own households, and in which the only individuals possibly over thirty are drunkards, jokesters, and gulls, totally without authority. All the external barriers to fulfillment have been eliminated in what becomes almost a parody of the state desired by the ordinary young lovers, the Hermias and Lysanders — or even the Rosalinds and Orlandos. According to the strictly romantic formula, the happy ending should be already achieved at the beginning of the play: we should abandon the theater for the rites of love. But the slightly stunned inhabitants of Illyria discover that they are anything but free. Their own actions provide the barriers, for most of them know neither themselves, nor others, nor their social world.

For his festival entertainment, Shakespeare freshly organized all the usual material of the romances — the twins, the exile, the impersonations — to provide significant movement for a dance of maskers. Every char-

From *The University of Kansas City Review*, XXII (1955), pp. 25–32. Copyright 1955 by the University of Kansas City. Reprinted by permission of the editor and the author.

acter has his mask, for the assumption of the play is that no one is with-out a mask in the serio-comic business of the pursuit of happiness. The character without disguises who is not ridiculous is outside the realm of comedy. Within comedy, the character who thinks it is possible to live without assuming a mask is merely too naive to recognize the mask he has already assumed. He is the chief object of laughter. As a general rule, we laugh with the characters who know the role they are playing and we laugh at those who do not; we can crudely divide the cast of *Twelfth Night* into those two categories.

But matters are more complicated than this, and roles have a way of shifting. All the butts except perhaps Sir Andrew Aguecheek have mo-ments in which they are the masters of our laughter; yet all the masters have moments in which they appear as fools. In our proper confusion, we must remember the alternative title of the play, "What You Will." It may indicate that everyone is free to invent his own title for the pro-ceedings. It also tells the author's intention to fulfill our desires: we wish to share in the triumphs of love and we wish to laugh; we wish our fools occasionally to be wise, and we are insistent that our wisest dra-matic figures experience our common fallibility. Most significantly, the title may hint that what "we" collectively "will" creates all the comic masks — that society determines the forms of comedy more directly than it determines those of any other literary genre.

At the opening of the play Orsino and Olivia accept the aristocratic (and literary) ideas of the romantic lover and the grief-stricken lady as realities rather than as ideas. They are comic characters exactly because of that confusion. Orsino glories in the proper moodiness and fickleness of the literary lover; only our own romanticism can bind us to the absurdities in his opening speech. Orsino first wishes the music to con-tinue so that the appetite of love may "surfeit"; immediately, however, he demands that the musicians stop the music they are playing to repeat an isolated phrase — an awkward procedure and a comic bit of stage business which is rarely utilized in productions. Four lines later the music must stop entirely because the repeated "strain" no longer *is* sweet, and the appetite is truly about to "surfeit." He then exclaims that the spirit of love is so "quick and fresh" that like the sea (hardly a model of freshness)

> naught enters there,
> Of what validity and pitch soe'er,
> But falls into abatement and low price,
> Even in a minute!

Orsino is a victim of a type of madness to which the most admirable characters are sometimes subject. Its usual causes are boredom, lack of physical love, and excessive imagination, and the victim is unaware that he is in love with love rather than with a person.

In the same scene, before we ever see the lady, Olivia's state is as nicely defined. Valentine, Orsino's messenger, has acquired something of his master's extraordinary language, and his report on his love mission manages both to please the Duke and to convey his own incredulity at the excess of Olivia's vow for her brother. In his speech the fresh and the salt are again confused. It is impossible to keep fresh something so ephemeral as grief; Olivia can make it last and "season" it, however, by the process of pickling — the natural effect of "eye-offending brine." Orsino feels unbounded admiration for the depth of soul indicated by Olivia's vow and at the same time he assumes that the vow can easily be broken by a lover. He departs for "sweet *beds of* flow'rs" which are somehow to provide a *canopy* for "love-thoughts."

Both Orsino and Olivia have adopted currently fashionable literary postures; yet neither of them is a fool. We are glad to be reassured by the Captain that Orsino is "A noble duke, in nature as in name," and that his present infatuation is only a month old. Sir Toby's later remark "What a plague means my niece, to take the death of her brother thus?" indicates that Olivia too had seemed an unlikely candidate for affectation. She is also an unconvincing practitioner. Although at our first glimpse of her she is properly the grief-stricken lady ("Take the fool away"), her propriety collapses under Feste's famous catechism. We discover that Olivia is already bored and that she really desires to love. Outraged nature has its full and comic revenge when Olivia falls passionately in love with a male exterior and acts with an aggressiveness which makes Orsino seem almost feminine. Still properly an actor in comedy, Olivia quickly changes from the character who has confused herself with a socially attractive mask to one who fails to perceive the mask which society has imposed on another.

Viola's situation allows time for neither love- nor grief-in-idleness. A virgin, shipwrecked in a strange land, possessing only wit and intelligence and the Captain's friendship, she must act immediately if she is to preserve herself. She, like Olivia, has "lost" a brother, but the luxury of conventional mourning is quickly exchanged for a *willed* hope that, as she was saved, "so perchance may he be." With Viola's wish for time to know what her "estate is," before she is "delivered to the world," we are reminded that society often requires a mask, neither for the relief of boredom nor the enjoyment of acting, but merely for self-preservation. While Antonio, "friend to Sebastian," almost loses his life because of his failure to assume a disguise, Viola suffers from no failure of discretion or imagination. She must assume a disguise as a boy and she must have help in preparing it.

Although she knows the ways of the world, Viola takes the necessary chance and wills to trust the Captain:

> There is a fair behavior in thee, Captain.
> And though that Nature with a beauteous wall
> Doth oft close in pollution, yet of thee
> I will believe thou hast a mind that suits
> With this thy fair and outward character.

We have in this second scene not only the beginning of one strand of the complicated intrigue, but also the creation of the one character active in the intrigue who provides a measure for the comic excesses of all the others. (Feste's role as observer is analogous to Viola's role as "actor.") Although Viola chooses to impersonate Cesario from necessity, she later plays her part with undisguised enjoyment. She misses none of the opportunities for parody, for confession, and for *double entendre* which the mask affords, and she never forgets or lets us forget the biological distance between Viola and Cesario. Except in the fencing match with Sir Andrew Aguecheek, she anticipates and directs our perception of the ludicrous in her own role as well as in the roles of Orsino and Olivia.

Sebastian is the reality of which Cesario is the artful imitation. Viola's twin assumes no disguise; Viola and the inhabitants of Illyria have assumed it for him. He is, to the eye, identical with Viola, and his early scenes with Antonio serve to remind us firmly of his existence as well as to introduce an initial exhilarating confusion at the entrance of either of the twins. When he truly enters the action of the play in Act IV he is certainly the object of our laughter, not because he has confused himself with an ideal or improper mask, but because he so righteously and ineffectually insists on his own identity in the face of unanimous public opposition. Our attitude quickly changes, however, to a mixture of amused patronization and identification: we do, after all, *know* so much more than does Sebastian; yet, within the context of the play, we can hardly keep from identifying with the gentleman who, practically if not idealistically, decides not to reject the reality of a passionate Olivia just because he has never seen her before:

> Or I am mad, or else this is a dream.
> Let fancy still my sense in Lethe steep.
> If it be thus to dream, still let me sleep!

The other characters in the play do not truly belong to an aristocracy of taste and leisure. For some of them, that is the chief problem. Malvolio and Sir Andrew Aguecheek are ruled by their mistaken notions of the proper role of an upper-class gentleman, and they fail to perceive the comic gaps between themselves and their ideal roles, and between those ideals and the social reality. Sick with self-love as he is, Malvolio is also sick with his desire to rise in society: "an affectioned ass, that cons state without book and utters it by great swaths: the best persuaded of himself, so crammed, as he thinks, with excellencies, that it is his grounds of faith that all that look on him love him." Although he knows it without, he has learned his "state" by book — but such a pupil inevitably distorts the text. He dreams of ruling a thrifty and solemn household while he plays with "some rich jewel," a dream characteristically attractive to the *arriviste* and absolutely impossible to the *arrivé.* We, like Maria, "can hardly forbear hurling things at him." His is as absurd as the reverse image which possesses Sir Andrew, a carpet-knight rightly described by Sir Toby as "an ass-head and a coxcomb and a knave, a thin-faced knave, a gull!" In the gallery of false images Sir Andrew's roaring boy hangs opposite Malvolio's burgher. Although in a low moment Sir Andrew may think that he has "no more wit than a Christian or an ordinary man has," he never has such grave self-doubt for long. Like a true gull, he tries to assume the particular role which, of all others, he is most poorly equipped to play: drinker, fighter, wencher.

Sir Andrew, however, would hardly exist without Sir Toby Belch: the gull must have his guller. Sir Toby may fulfill Sir Andrew's idea of what a gentleman should be, but Sir Toby himself has no such odd idea of gentility. (Sir Andrew may be "a dear manikin to you, Sir Toby," but Sir Toby has a superlatively good reason for allowing him to be: "I have been dear to him, lad, some two thousand strong, or so.") Even at his most drunken, we are delightfully unsure whether we laugh at or with Sir Toby, whether he is or is not fully conscious of the effects as well as the causes of his "mistakes," his verbal confusions, and even his belches. Like another drunken knight, and like Viola, Toby possesses a range of dramatic talents and he enjoys using them. He is equally effective as the fearless man of action, as the practitioner of noble "gentleness" with the "mad" Malvolio, and as the experienced alcoholic guide to Sir Andrew. His joy is in the jest as well as in the bottle, and he can bring himself to abandon the latter long enough to marry Maria simply in admiration for her ability as an intriguer. But like other knowing players, Sir Toby is vulnerable to deception. He is object rather than master of our laughter from the time when he mistakes Sebastian for Cesario and attempts to assert his masculine ability as a swordsman.

In the business of masking, ~~Feste~~ is the one professional among a crowd of amateurs; he does it for a living. He never makes the amateur's mistake of confusing his personality with his mask — he wears not motley in his brain. Viola recognizes his wisdom and some kinship in the fact that each "must observe their mood on whom he jests." But though Feste may have deliberately chosen his role, society determines its conditions. Now that he is growing old, the conditions become difficult: "Go to, you're a dry fool, I'll no more of you. Besides, you grow dishonest." While all the other characters are concerned with gaining something they do not have, Feste's struggle is to retain his mask and to make it again ingratiating. He is able to penetrate all the masks of the others and he succeeds in retaining his own.

However fanciful its dreams of desire, the play moves within a context of an almost real world, from one disguise and half-understood intrigue to another, until all its elements are whirled into a complexly related and moving figure. With the constant contrasts and parallels and reversals in character, situation, and intrigue, we find ourselves at last, along with Malvolio and Olivia and Viola and the rest, in a state of real delirium. Until the concluding scene, however, we can largely agree with Sebastian: if we dream, we do not wish to wake; if this is madness, it is still comic madness, and we do not envy the sane. The attempts at false and inflexible authority are being defeated, the pretentious are being deflated, and the very sentimentality of the likeable sentimentalists has led them close to biological reality. We are particularly delighted with Viola. Young, intelligent, zestful, she is a realist. She cuts through the subterfuges and disguises of the others with absolute clarity, and she provides us with a center for the movement, a standard of normality which is never dull. In her rejection of the artificial myths of love, moreover, Viola never becomes the advocate of a far more terrifying myth, the myth of absolute rationality. In a completely rational world, Shakespeare never tires of pointing out, what we know as love could not exist. We have never desired such a world.

From the time of her first aside to the audience after she has seen Orsino ("Yet a barful strife!/Whoe'er I woo, myself would be his wife"), Viola directly admits her irrational love. She differs, then, from Orsino and Olivia not in any invulnerability to blindness and passion, but in the clarity and simplicity with which she recognizes and accepts her state. Reason is not abandoned: she rationally admits her irrationality and her inability to cope with the situation:

> O Time, thou must untangle this, not I!
> It is too hard a knot for me to untie!

Viola needs a miracle. Although she may imagine herself as "Patience on a monument, smiling at grief," she remains as close as possible to her loved one and waits for the miracle to happen. Since we have seen Sebastian, we know that the miracle will occur; yet through our identification with Viola we come to know the comic burden, the masker's increasing weariness of the mask which implies that love is still pursued rather than possessed.

The burden becomes comically unbearable only in the final scene, when it is cast off. Here Shakespeare underscores all those possibilities of violence and death which are usually submerged in comedy. Antonio is arrested and in danger of his life. Orsino, finally recognizing the hopelessness of his suit to Olivia, shows the vicious side of sentimentality. After considering the possibility of killing Olivia "like to the Egyptian thief," he determines to do violence to "Cesario":

> Come, boy, with me. My thoughts are ripe in mischief.
> I'll sacrifice the lamb that I do love,
> To spite a raven's heart within a dove.

Olivia is hysterical at what seems to be the baseness of Cesario. Sir Toby has a broken pate to show for his one major failure to penetrate a mask. The dance must stop. The miracle must occur.

The entrance of Sebastian is "what we will." It is the most dramatic moment of the play. The confrontation of Sebastian and Cesario-Viola, those identical images, concludes the formal plot and provides the means for the discarding of all the lovers' masks. The moment must be savored and fully realized. As Viola and Sebastian chant their traditional formulas of proof, both the audience and the other characters on the stage undistractedly view the physical image of the duality which has made the confusion and the play. The masks and the play are to be abandoned for a vision of delight beyond delight, in which lovers have neither to wear nor to penetrate disguises since they are at last invulnerable to error and laughter.

Yet the play does not resolve into a magic blessing of the world's fertility as does *A Midsummer Night's Dream*. We have been promised a happy ending, and we receive it. We are grateful that the proper Jacks and Jills have found each other, but the miracle is a limited miracle, available only to the young and the lucky. Not every Jack has his Jill even in Illyria, and after the general unmasking, those without love may seem even lonelier. Malvolio, of course, is justly punished. He has earned his mad scene, and with the aid of Feste he has made it comic. As a result of his humiliation he has also earned some sort of redress. Yet he is ridiculous in his arrogance to the end, and his threatened revenge, now that he is powerless to effect it, sustains the comedy and the characterization and prevents the obtrusion of destructive pathos.

It is Feste rather than Malvolio who finally reminds us of the limitations and the costs of the romantic vision of happiness with which we have been seduced. However burdensome, masking is his career, and romantic love provides no end for it. Alone on the stage at the end of the play, he sings a song of unfulfilled love which shows the other side of the coin. For Feste, as for his audience, the mask can never be finally discarded: the rain it raineth every day. His song has those overtones, I believe, but they are only overtones. The music, here and elsewhere in the play, provides an element in which oppositions may be resolved. And the song itself, like the movement which must accompany it, is crude and witty as well as graceful and nostalgic. However far it may have missed the conventionally happy ending, Feste's saga of misfortunes in love is comic, even from his own point of view. The exaggeration so often operative in the refrains of Elizabethan lyrics emphasizes that the watery as well as the sunny vision can become funny: it doesn't rain every day by a long shot.

The song, which begins as the wittiest observer's comment on the denouement of the play, ends as a dissolution of the dramatic fiction:

> A great while ago the world begun,
> With hey, ho, the wind and the rain,
> But that's all one, our play is done,
> And we'll strive to please you every day.

The audience has been a participant in the festivity. As the fictional lovers have unmasked to reveal or realize their "true" identities, it is only proper that the clown, the only character who might move freely in the environs of Bankside, as well as in the realm of Illyria, should unmask the whole proceeding for the imitation of a desired world which it has been. The audience must be returned from "What You Will" to its own less patterned world where the sea rarely disgorges siblings given up for lost, where mistaken marriages rarely turn out well, where Violas rarely catch Dukes, and where Malvolios too often rule households with disturbing propriety. The lovers have met, and Feste announces that present laughter has come to an end. But the actors, those true and untiring maskers, will continue to "strive to please" us. They will find few occasions in the future in which their efforts will be more sure of success.

Twelfth Night is the climax of Shakespeare's early achievement in comedy. The effects and values of the earlier comedies are here subtly embodied in the most complex structure which Shakespeare had yet created. But the play also looks forward: the pressure to dissolve the comedy, to realize and finally abandon the burden of laughter, is an intrinsic part of its "perfection." Viola's clear-eyed and affirmative vision of her own and the world's irrationality is a triumph and we desire it; yet we realize its vulnerability, and we come to realize that virtue in disguise is only totally triumphant when evil is not in disguise — is not truly present at all. Having solved magnificently the problems of this particular form of comedy, Shakespeare was evidently not tempted to repeat his triumph. After *Twelfth Night* the so-called comedies require for their happy resolution more radical characters and devices — omniscient and omnipresent Dukes, magic, and resurrection. More obvious miracles are needed for comedy to exist in a world in which evil also exists, not merely incipiently but with power.

JOHN HOLLANDER

Twelfth Night and
The Morality of Indulgence

To SAY THAT a play is "moral" would seem to imply that it represents
an action which concretizes certain ethical elements of human experience. It need not actually moralize at any point, nor need any of the
characters in it state univocally a dogma, precept, or value that would
coincide completely with the play's own moral intention. It was just
this univocal didacticism, however, which characterized what was becoming in 1600 a prevailing comic tradition. The moral intent of the
Jonsonian "comedy of humours" was direct and didactic; its purpose
was to show

> the times deformitie
> Anatomiz'd in euery nerue and sinnew
> With constant courage, and contempt of feare.[1]

For moral purposes, a humour is an identifying emblem of a man's moral
nature, graven ineradicably onto his physiological one. In the world of
a play, a humour could be caricatured to such a degree that it would
practically predestine a character's behavior. It was made to

> . . . so possesse a man, that it doth draw
> All his affects, his spirits and his powers,
> In their confluctions, all to runne one way,
> This may be truly said to be a Humour.

The emblematic character of the humour, and the necessity for its
use, were affirmed even more directly by Sidney, whose dramatic theory
Jonson seems to have greatly admired.

From *The Sewanee Review*, LXVII (1959), pp. 220–238. Copyright by The University of
the South. Reprinted by permission of the author and the publisher. The author has made
minor changes in the original article for this edition.

[1] Ben Jonson, *Every Man Out of His Humour* (1599), Induction, 11. 120–122.

Now *Every Man In His Humour* was first acted in 1598, and it is known that Shakespeare appeared in it. He seems in *Twelfth Night* (for which I accept the traditional date of 1600–1601) to have attempted to write a kind of moral comedy diametrically opposed to that of Jonson, in which "the times deformitie" was not to be "anatomiz'd," but represented in the core of an action. For a static and deterministic Humour, Shakespeare substituted a kinetic, governing Appetite in the action, rather than in the bowels, of his major characters. In his plot and language, he insists continually on the fact and importance of the substitution. Characters in a comedy of humours tend to become caricatures, and caricatures tend to become beasts, inhuman personifications of moral distortions that are identified with physiological ones. I believe that it was Shakespeare's intention in *Twelfth Night* to obviate the necessity of this dehumanization by substituting what one might call a moral process for a moral system. While it is true that the play contains quite a bit of interesting discussion of humours as such, and that there is some correspondence between appetites and humours, it is equally true that the only person in the play who believes in the validity of humourous classifications, who, indeed, lives by them, is himself a moral invalid. I will have more to say about this later. At this point I merely wish to suggest that the primary effective difference between Shakespeare's and Jonson's techniques in making moral comedy is the difference between what is merely a display of anatomy, and a dramatization of a metaphor, the difference between a Pageant and an Action.

II

The Action of *Twelfth Night* is indeed that of a Revels, a suspension of mundane affairs during a brief epoch in a temporary world of indulgence, a land full of food, drink, love, play, disguise and music. But parties end, and the reveller eventually becomes satiated and drops heavily into his worldly self again. The fact that plays were categorized as "revells" for institutional purposes may have appealed to Shakespeare; he seems at any rate to have analyzed the dramatic and moral nature of feasting, and to have made it the subject of his play. His analysis is schematized in Orsino's opening speech.

The essential action of a revels is: To so surfeit the Appetite upon excess that it "may sicken and so die." It is the Appetite, not the whole Self, however, which is surfeited: the Self will emerge at the conclusion of the action from where it has been hidden. The movement of the play is toward this emergence of humanity from behind a mask of comic type.

Act I, Scene 1, is very important as a statement of the nature of this movement. Orsino's opening line contains the play's three dominant images:

> If music be the food of love, play on.
> Give me excess of it, that, surfeiting,
> The appetite may sicken, and so die.   (I. i. 1–3)

Love, eating, and music are the components of the revelry, then. And in order that there be no mistake about the meaning of the action, we get a miniature rehearsal of it following immediately:

> That strain again! It had a dying fall.
> Oh, it came o'er my ear like the sweet sound
> That breathes upon a bank of violets
> Stealing and giving odor! Enough, no more.
> 'Tis not so sweet now as it was before.
> O spirit of love, how quick and fresh art thou!
> That, notwithstanding thy capacity
> Receiveth as the sea, naught enters there,
> Of what validity and pitch soe'er,
> But falls into abatement and low price,
> Even in a minute! So full of shapes is fancy
> That it alone is high fantastical.   (I. i. 4–15)

A bit of surfeiting is actually accomplished here; what we are getting is a proem to the whole play, and a brief treatment of love as an appetite. The substance of a feast will always fall into "abatement and low price" at the conclusion of the feasting, for no appetite remains to demand it. We also think of Viola in connection with the "violets/ Stealing and giving odor," for her actual position as go-between-turned-lover is one of both inadvertent thief and giver. The Duke's rhetoric is all-embracing, however, and he immediately comments significantly upon his own condition.

> Or, when mine eyes did see Olivia first,
> Methought she purged the air of pestilence!
> That instant was I turned into a hart,
> And my desires, like fell and cruel hounds,
> E'er since pursue me.   (I. i. 19–23)

Like Actaeon, he is the hunter hunted; the active desirer pursued by his own desires. As embodying this overpowering appetite for romantic love, he serves as a host of the revels.[2]

The other host is Olivia, the subject of his desire. We see almost at once that her self-indulgence is almost too big to be encompassed by

[2] See the extremely provocative commentary on the Duke's opening lines in Kenneth Burke, *The Philosophy of Literary Form* (Baton Rouge, 1941), pp. 344–349.

Orsino's. Valentine, reporting on the failure of his mission, describes her state as follows:

> So please my lord, I might not be admitted,
> But from her handmaid do return this answer:
> The element itself, till seven years' heat,
> Shall not behold her face at ample view;
> But, like a cloistress, she will veiled walk
> And water once a day her chamber round
> With eye-offending brine — all this to season
> A brother's dead love, which she would keep fresh
> And lasting in her sad remembrance. (I. i. 24–32)

"To season a brother's dead love": she is gorging herself on this fragrant herb, and though she has denied herself the world, she is no true anchorite, but, despite herself, a private glutton. The Duke looks forward to the end of her feast of grief,

> . . . when liver, brain, and heart,
> These sovereign thrones, are all supplied, and filled
> Her sweet perfections with one self king! (I. i. 37–39)

The trinitarian overtone is no blasphemy, but a statement of the play's teleology. When everyone is supplied with "one self king," the action will have been completed.

The first three scenes of the play stand together as a general prologue, in which the major characters are introduced and their active natures noted. Viola is juxtaposed to Olivia here; she is not one to drown her own life in a travesty of mourning. It is true that she is tempted to "serve that lady" (as indeed she does, in a different way). But her end in so doing would be the whole play's action in microcosm; the immersion in committed self-indulgence would result in the revelation of her self:

> And might not be delivered to the world
> Till I had made mine own occasion mellow,
> What my estate is. (I. ii. 42–44)

She will serve the Duke instead, and use her persuasive talents to accomplish the ends to which his own self-celebrating rhetoric can provide no access. "I can sing," she says, "and speak to him in many sorts of music." Her sense of his character has been verified; the Captain tells her that his name is as his nature. And "what is his name?" she asks. "Orsino," answers the Captain. Orsino — the bear, the ravenous and clumsy devourer. Her own name suggests active, affective music;

and the mention of Arion, the Orpheus-like enchanter of waves and dolphins with his music, points up the connotation. Orsino's "music," on the other hand, is a static well of emotion in which he allows his own rhetoric to submerge; Viola's is more essentially instrumental, effective, and convincing.[3]

The third scene of Act I completes the prologue by further equating the moral and the physiological. Here we first encounter the world of what Malvolio calls "Sir Toby and the lighter people" (it is indeed true that there is none of Malvolio's element of "earth" in them). The continued joking about *dryness* that pervades the wit here in Olivia's house, both above and below stairs, is introduced here, in contrast to Olivia's floods of welling and self-indulgent tears. The idea behind the joking in this and the following scenes is that drinking and merriment will moisten and fulfill a dry nature. As Feste says later on, "Give the dry fool drink, then the fool is not dry." Toby's sanguine temperament and Aguecheek's somewhat phlegmatic one are here unveiled. They are never identified as such, however; and none of the wit that is turned on the associations of "humours," "elements" and "waters," though it runs throughout the play, ever refers to a motivating order in the universe, except insofar as Malvolio believes in it.

What is most important is that neither Feste, the feaster embodying not the spirit but the action of revelry, nor Malvolio, the ill-wisher (and the *bad appetite* as well), his polar opposite, appears in these introductory scenes. It is only upstairs in Olivia's house (I, v) that the action as such commences. The revel opens with Feste's exchange with Maria in which she attempts three times to insist on innocent interpretations of "well-hanged" and "points." But Feste is resolute in his ribaldry. Thus Olivia, momentarily voicing Malvolio's invariable position, calls Feste a "dry fool," and "dishonest"; Malvolio himself refers to him as a "barren rascal." From here on in it will be Feste who dances attendance on the revelry, singing, matching wit with Viola, and being paid by almost everyone for his presence. To a certain degree he remains outside the action, not participating in it because he represents its very nature; occasionally serving as a comic angel or messenger, he is nevertheless unmotivated by any appetite, and is never sated of his fooling. His insights into the action are continuous, and his every remark is telling. "*Cucullus non facit monachum.* That's as much as to say I wear not motley in my brain."[4] Indeed, he does not, but more important is the

---

3 See my own "Musica Mundana and Twelfth Night" in *Sound and Poetry*, ed. Northrop Frye (New York, 1957), pp. 55–82, for an extended treatment of the use of "speculative" and "practical" music in the play.

4 Cf. *Measure for Measure*, V, i, 263, where Lucio refers in the identical words to the Duke disguised as Friar Lodowick.

fact that his robe and beard are not to make him a *real* priest later on. And neither he as Sir Thopas, nor Olivia as a "cloistress," nor Malvolio in his black suit of travestied virtue, nor the transvestite Viola is what he appears to be. No one will be revealed in his true dress until he has doffed his mask of feasting. And although neither Feste nor Malvolio will change in this respect, it is for completely opposite reasons that they will not do so.

Every character in the play, however, is granted some degree of insight into the nature of the others. It is almost as if everyone were masked with the black side of his vizard turned inwards; he sees more clearly past the *persona* of another than he can past his own. Valentine, for the Duke, comments on Olivia, as we have seen before. Even Malvolio is granted such an insight. Olivia asks him "What manner of man" Caesario is; unwittingly, his carping, over self-conscious and intellectualized answer cuts straight to the heart of Viola's disguise: "Not yet old enough for a man, nor young enough for a boy, as a squash is before 'tis a peascod, or a codling when 'tis almost an apple. 'Tis with him in standing water, between boy and man. He is very well-favored and he speaks very shrewishly. One would think his mother's milk were scarce out of him." (I. v. 165–171)

The puns on "cod" and "codling" insist on being heard here, and as with the inadvertently delivered obscenity about Olivia's "great P's" and their source in the letter scene, Malvolio does not know what he is saying. The point is that Malvolio asserts, for an audience that knows the real facts, that Viola can scarcely be a male creature.

A more significant case of this hide-and-seek is Olivia's retort to Malvolio in the same scene: "O you are sick of self-love, Malvolio, and taste with a distempered appetite"; it provides the key to his physio-logical-moral nature. "Sick of self-love" means "sick with a moral infection called self-love," but it can also mean "already surfeited, or fed up with your own ego as an object of appetite." Malvolio's "distem-pered appetite" results from the fact that he alone is not possessed of a craving directed outward, towards some object on which it can surfeit and die; he alone cannot morally benefit from a period of self-indulgence. Actually this distemper manifests itself in terms of transitory desires on his part for status and for virtue, but these desires consume him in their fruitlessness; he is aware of the nature of neither of them. This is a brilliant analysis of the character of a melancholic, and Shakespeare's association of the melancholy, puritanic and status-seeking characters in Malvolio throws considerable light on all of them. The moral nature of the plot of *Twelfth Night* can be easily approached through the char-acter of Malvolio, and this, I think, is what Lamb and his followers missed completely in their egalitarian sympathy for his being no "more than steward." For Malvolio's attachment to self-advancement is not being either aristocratically ridiculed or praised as an example of righteous bourgeois opposition to medieval hierarchies. In the context of the play's moral physiology, his disease is shown forth as a case of indigestion due to his self-love, the result of a perverted, rather than an excessive appetite.[5] In the world of feasting, the values of the commercial society outside the walls of the party go topsy-turvy: Feste is given money for making verbal fools of the donors thereof; everyone's desire is fulfilled in an unexpected way; and revellers are shown to rise through realms of unreality, disguise and luxurious self-deception. We are seduced, by the revelling, away from seeing the malice in the plot to undo Malvolio. But whatever malice there is remains peculiarly just. It is only Malvolio who bears any ill-will, and only he upon whom ill-will can appear to be directed. He makes for himself a hell of the worldly heaven of festivity, and when Toby and Maria put him into darkness, into a counterfeit-hell, they are merely representing in play a condition that he has already achieved.

The plot against Malvolio, then, is no more than an attempt to let him surfeit on himself, to present him with those self-centered, "time-pleasing" objects upon which his appetite is fixed. In essence, he is led to a feast in which his own vision of himself is spread before him, and commanded to eat it. The puritan concern with witchcraft and the satanic, and its associations of them with madness are carried to a logical extreme; and once Malvolio has been permitted to indulge in his self-interest by means of the letter episode, he is only treated as he would himself treat anyone whom he believed to be mad. His puritanism is mocked by allusions to his praying made by Toby and Maria; a priest (and a false, dissembling one at that, the answer to a puritan's prayer) is sent to him; and the implications of the darkness are eventually fulfilled as his prison becomes his hell.

It is interesting to notice how carefully Shakespeare analyzed another characteristic of the melancholic in his treatment of Malvolio. L. C. Knights has suggested[6] that the vogue of melancholy at the turn of the 17th century was occasioned to some degree by the actual presence in England of a large number of "intellectuels en chômage" (in Denis de Rougement's words), unemployed, university-trained men whose humanistic education had not fitted them for any suitable role in society. Malvolio is no patent and transparent university intellectual (like Holofernes, for example). He contrives, however, to over-rationalize his

---

5 And Leslie Hotson has pointed out that his yellow stockings, as he later appears in them, are the true color of the Narcissus, as well as of the craven. See The First Night of Twelfth Night (London, 1954), p. 98f.

6 Drama and Society in the Age of Jonson (Manchester, 1936), pp. 315–332.

point (where the Duke will over-sentimentalize it) on almost every occasion. Even his first introduction of Viola, as has been seen before, is archly over-reasoned. His venture into exegesis of a text is almost telling.

It is not merely self-interest, I think, that colors the scrutiny of Maria's letter. His reading is indeed a close one: he observes that, after the first snatch of doggerel, "The numbers altered." But Malvolio is incapable of playing the party-game and guessing the riddle. Of "M, O, A, I doth sway my life," he can only say "And yet, to crush this a little it would bow to me, for every one of these letters are in my name." He even avoids the reading that should, by all rights, appeal to him: Leslie Hotson has suggested that "M, O, A, I" probably stands for *Mare, Orbis, Aer* and *Ignis,* the four elements to which Malvolio so often refers. Malvolio himself fails as a critic, following a "cold scent" that, as Fabian indicates, is "as rank as a fox" for him in that it tantalizes his ambition.

But he continues to aspire to scholarship. In order to "let his tongue tang" with arguments of state, he intends to "read politic authors." His intrusion on the scene of Toby's and Andrew's merry-making involves a most significant remark: "Is there no respect of persons, time or place in you?," he asks. In other words, "Do you not observe even the dramatic unities in your revelling? Can you not apply even the values that govern things as frivolous as plays to your lives?" Coming from Malvolio, the ethical theorist, the remark feels very different from the remark made to Sir Toby by Maria, the practical moralist: "Aye, but you must confine yourself within the modest levels of order." Maria, presiding over the festivities, would keep things from getting out of hand. It is not only the spirit in which Malvolio's comment is uttered that accounts for this difference, however. I think that one of the implications is quite clearly the fact that Jonson's ordered, would-be-classic, but static and didactic comedy would disapprove of *Twelfth Night* as a moral play, and mistake its intention for a purely frivolous one.

The prank played on Malvolio is not merely an "interwoven" second story, but a fully-developed double-plot. Like the Belmont episodes in *The Merchant of Venice,* it is a condensed representation of the action of the entire play. In *Twelfth Night,* however, it operates in reverse, to show the other side of the coin, as it were. For Malvolio there can be no fulfillment in "one self king." His story effectively and ironically underlines the progress toward this fulfillment in everybody else, and helps to delineate the limitations of the moral domain of the whole play. In contrast to Feste, who appears in the action at times as an abstracted spirit of revelry, Malvolio is a model of the sinner.

The whole play abounds in such contrasts and parallels of character, and the players form and regroup continually with respect to these, much in the manner of changing of figurations in a suite of *branles*. Viola herself indulges in the festivities in a most delicate and (literally) charming way. She is almost too good a musician, too effective an Orpheus: "Heaven forbid my outside have not charmed her," she complains after her first encounter with Olivia. But as soon as she realizes that she is part of the game, she commits herself to it with redoubled force. If her "outside" is directed towards Olivia, her real identity and her own will are concentrated even more strongly on Orsino. In the most ironic of the love-scenes, she all but supplants Olivia in the Duke's affections. Orsino, glutting himself on his own version of romantic love, allows himself to make the most extravagant and self-deceptive statements about it:

> Come hither, boy. If ever thou shalt love,
> In the sweet pangs of it remember me;
> For such as I am all true lovers are,
> Unstaid and skittish in all motions else
> Save in the constant image of the creature
> That is beloved. (II. iv. 15–20)

This skittishness, beneath the mask of the ravenous and constant bear, is obvious to Feste, at least: "Now, the melancholy god protect thee, and the tailor make thy doublet of changeable taffeta, for thy mind is a very opal. I would have men of such constancy put to sea, that their business might be everything and their intent everywhere; for that's it that always makes a good voyage of nothing." (II. iv. 75–80)

Orsino also gives us a curious version of the physiology of the passions on which the plot is based; it is only relatively accurate, of course, for he will be the last of the revellers to feel stuffed, to push away from him his heaping dish.

> There is no woman's sides
> Can bide the beating of so strong a passion
> As love doth give my heart, no woman's heart
> So big to hold so much. They lack retention.
> Alas, their love may be called appetite —
> No motion of the liver, but the palate —
> They suffer surfeit, cloyment and revolt.
> But mine is all as hungry as the sea
> And can digest as much. (II. iv. 96–104)

Viola has been giving him her "inside" throughout the scene, and were he not still ravenous for Olivia's love he could see her for what she is: a woman with a constancy in love (for himself and her brother) that he can only imagine himself to possess. She is indeed an Allegory of

Patience on some baroque tomb at this point. She is ironically distinguished from Olivia in that her "smiling at grief" is a disguising "outside" for her real sorrow, whereas Olivia's is a real self-indulgent pleasure taken at a grief outworn. It is as if Olivia had misread Scripture and taken the letter of "Blessed are they that mourn" for the spirit of it. Her grief is purely ceremonial.

The "lighter people," too, are engaged in carrying out the action in their own way, and they have more business in the play than merely to make a gull of Malvolio. Toby's huge stomach for food and drink parallels the Duke's ravenous capacity for sentiment. The drinking scene is in one sense the heart of the play. It starts out by declaring itself in no uncertain terms. "Does not our life consist of the four elements?" catechizes Sir Toby. "Faith, so they say," replies Andrew, "but I think it rather consists of eating and drinking." No one but Feste, perhaps, really knows the extent to which this is true, for Andrew is actually saying "We are not merely comic types, mind you, being manipulated by a dramatist of the humours. The essence of our lives lies in a movement from hunger to satiety that we share with all of nature."

When Toby and Andrew cry out for a love song, Feste obliges them, not with the raucous and bawdy thing that one would expect, but instead, with a direct appeal to their actual hostess, Olivia. This is all the more remarkable in that it is made on behalf of everyone in the play. "O Mistress Mine" undercuts the Duke's overwhelming but ineffectual mouthings, Viola's effective but necessarily misdirected charming, and, of course, Aguecheek's absolute incompetence as a suitor. The argument is couched in purely naturalistic terms: "This feast will have to end, and so will all of our lives. You are not getting younger ('sweet and twenty' is the contemporaneous equivalent of 'sweet and thirty,' at least). Give up this inconstant roaming; your little game had better end in your marriage, anyway." The true love "That can sing both high and low" is Viola-Sebastian, the master-mistress of Orsino's and Olivia's passion. (Sebastian has just been introduced in the previous scene, and there are overtones here of his being invoked as Olivia's husband). Sebastian has, aside from a certain decorative but benign courtly manner, no real identity apart from Viola. He is the fulfillment of her longing (for she has thought him dead) and the transformation into reality of the part she is playing in the *ludus amoris*. The prognostication is borne out by Sebastian's own remark: "You are betrothed both to a man and maid." He is himself characterized by an elegance hardly virile; and, finally, we must keep in mind the fact that Viola was played by a boy actor to begin with, and that Shakespeare's audience seemed to be always ready for an intricate irony of this kind.

But if Viola and Sebastian are really the same, "One face, one voice, one habit, and two persons, A natural perspective that is and is not," there is an interesting parallel between Viola and Aguecheek as well. Both are suitors for Olivia's hand: Andrew, ineffectively, for himself; Viola for Orsino, and (effectively) for Sebastian. Their confrontation in the arranged duel is all the more ironic in that Andrew is an effective pawn in Toby's game (Toby is swindling him), whereas Viola is an ineffective one in the Duke's (she is swindling him of Olivia's love).

Feste's other songs differ radically from "O Mistress Mine." He sings for the Duke a kind of languorous ayre, similar to so many that one finds in the songbooks.[7] It is aimed at Orsino in the very extravagance of its complaint. It is his own song, really, if we imagine him suddenly dying of love, being just as ceremoniously elaborate in his funeral instructions as he has been in his suit of Olivia. And Feste's bit of handy-dandy to Malvolio in his prison is a rough-and-tumble sort of thing, intended to suggest in its measures a scrap from a Morality, plainly invoking Malvolio in darkness as a devil in hell. Feste shows himself throughout the play to be a master of every convention of fooling.

If Feste's purpose is to serve as a symbol of the revels, however, he must also take a clear and necessary part in the all-important conclusion. *Twelfth Night* itself, the feast of the Epiphany, celebrates the discovery of the "True King" in the manger by the Wise Men. "Those wits," says Feste in Act I, Scene 5 "that think they have thee [wit] do very oft prove fools, and I that am sure I lack thee may pass for a wise man." And so it is that under his influence the true Caesario, the "one self king," is revealed.[8] The whole of Act V might be taken, in connection with "the plot" in a trivial sense, to be the other *epiphany,* the perception that follows the *anagnorisis* or discovery of classic dramaturgy. But we have been dealing with the Action of *Twelfth Night* as representing the killing off of excessive appetite through indulgence of it, leading to the rebirth of the unencumbered self. The long final scene, then, serves to show forth the Caesario-King, and to unmask, discover and reveal the fulfilled selves in the major characters.

The appearance of the priest (a real one, this time) serves more than the simple purpose of proving the existence of a marriage between Olivia and "Caesario." It is a simple but firm intrusion into the world of the play of a way of life that has remained outside of it so far. The straightforward solemnity of the priest's rhetoric is also something new; suggestions of its undivided purpose have appeared before only in

7 The Rev. E. H. Fellowes, in *English Madrigal Verse* (Oxford, 1929), lists four different ayres with the conventional opening phrase, "Come away."

8 For my interpretation of the last act I am indebted to Professor Roy W. Battenhouse's suggestions.

Antonio's speeches. The priest declares that Olivia and her husband have been properly married:

> And all the ceremony of this compact
> Sealed in my function, by my testimony.
> Since when, my watch hath told me, toward my grave
> I have travelled but two hours.   (V. i. 163–166)

It is possible that the original performances had actually taken about two hours to reach this point. At any rate, the sombre acknowledgment of the passage of time in a real world is there. Antonio has prepared the way earlier in the scene; his straightforward confusion is that of the unwitting intruder in a masquerade who has been accused of mistaking the identities of two of the masquers.

That the surfeiting has gradually begun to occur, however, has become evident earlier. In the prison scene, Sir Toby has already begun to tire: "I would we were well rid of this knavery." He gives as his excuse for this the fact that he is already in enough trouble with Olivia, but such as this has not deterred him in the past. And, in the last scene, very drunk as he must be, he replies to Orsino's inquiry as to his condition that he hates the surgeon, "a drunken rogue." Self-knowledge has touched Sir Toby. He could not have said this earlier.

As the scene plays itself out, Malvolio alone is left unaccounted for. There is no accounting for him here, though; he remains a bad taste in the mouth. "Alas poor fool," says Olivia, "How have they baffled thee!" And thus, in Feste's words, "the whirligig of time brings in his revenges." Malvolio has become the fool, the "barren rascal." He leaves in a frenzy, to "be revenged," he shouts, "on the whole pack of you." He departs from the world of this play to resume a role in another, perhaps. His business has never been with the feasting to begin with, and now that it is over, and the revellers normalized, he is revealed as the true madman. He is "The Madly-Used Malvolio" to the additional degree that his own uses have been madness.

For Orsino and Viola the end has also arrived. She will be "Orsino's mistress and his fancy's queen." He has been surfeited of his misdirected voracity; the rich golden shaft, in his own words, "hath killed the flock of all affections else" that live in him. "Liver, brain and heart" are indeed all supplied; for both Olivia and himself, there has been fulfillment in "one self king." And, lest there be no mistake, each is to be married to a Caesario or king. Again, "Liver, brain and heart" seems to encompass everybody: Toby and Maria are married, Aguecheek chastened, etc.

At the end of the scene, all exit. Only Feste, the pure fact of feasting, remains. His final song is a summation of the play in many ways at once. Its formal structure seems to be a kind of quick rehearsal of the

Ages of Man. In youth, "A foolish thing was but a toy": the fool's bauble, emblematic of both his *membrum virile* and his trickery, is a trivial fancy. But in "man's estate," the bauble represents a threat of knavery and thievery to respectable society, who shuts its owner out of doors. The "swaggering" and incessant drunkenness of the following strophes bring Man into prime and dotage, respectively. Lechery, trickery, dissembling and drunkenness, inevitable and desperate in mundane existence, however, are just those activities which, mingled together in a world of feasting, serve to purge Man of the desire for them. The wind and the rain accompany him throughout his life, keeping him indoors with "dreams and imaginations" as a boy, pounding and drenching him unmercifully, when he is locked out of doors, remaining eternal and inevitable throughout his pride in desiring to perpetuate himself. The wind and the rain are the most desperate of elements, that pound the walls and batter the roof of the warm house that shuts them out, while, inside it, the revels are in progress. Only after the party is ended can Man face them without desperation.

It is the metaphor of the rain that lasts longest, though, and it recapitulates the images of water, elements and humours that have pervaded the entire play. Feste himself, who tires of nothing, addresses Viola: "Who you are and what you would are out of my welkin — I might say 'element' but the word is overworn." He adroitly comments on Malvolio's line "Go to; I am not of your element" by substituting a Saxon word for a Latin one. The additional association of the four elements with the humours cannot be overlooked. It is only Malvolio, of course, who uses the word "humour" with any seriousness: "And then to have the humour of State," he muses, as he imagines himself "Count Malvolio." Humours are also waters, however. And *waters*, or fluids of all kinds, are continually being forced on our attention. Wine, tears, seawater, even urine, are in evidence from the first scene on, and they are always being metaphorically identified with one another. They are all fluids, bathing the world of the play in possibilities for change as the humours do the body. Feste's answer to Maria in the prison scene has puzzled many editors; if we realize, however, that Feste is probably hysterically laughing at what he has just been up to, "Nay, I'm for all waters" may have the additional meaning that he is on the verge of losing control of himself. He is "for all waters" primarily in that he represents the fluidity of revelling celebration. And finally, when all is done, "The rain it raineth every day," and Feste reverts to gnomic utterance in a full and final seriousness. Water is rain that falls to us from Heaven. The world goes on. Our revels now are ended, but the actors solidify into humanity, in this case. "But that's all one, our play is done/ And we'll strive to please you every day."

NORTHROP FRYE

Comic Myth in Shakespeare

THE ELIZABETHAN age evolved two kinds of comedy, and the names of Ben Jonson and Shakespeare may be taken to typify each kind. Jonson's great comedies are comedies of manners: they are not exactly realistic plays, but they do maintain a kind of realistic illusion. No character or incident is introduced which permanently upsets that illusion, and unities of time and place are observed, not out of pedantry, but because they are essential to the unity of action. Shakespeare, on the other hand, never wrote a pure comedy of manners, and never failed to include something in his comedy which tends to dispel the realistic atmosphere. If there are no fairies or magical forests and islands, there are plot-themes derived from myth, folklore, and romance. The strong element of folklore in the baiting of Falstaff seems to me to rule out even *The Merry Wives*, which would otherwise be Shakespeare's closest approach to the Jonsonian formula. The unities of time and place largely disappear along with the unity of probability. They are observed in *The Tempest*, but *The Winter's Tale*, which belongs to the same late period, seems to make something of a point of defying them.

Jonson, of course, had a theory of comedy that was closely related to the critical canons of his time. He was doing everything that a Renaissance critic would mean by following nature. In his preface to *The Alchemist* he congratulates himself on his superiority to certain other writers of comedy, who, unlike him, "run away from nature." In his introduction to *Bartholomew Fair*, he is a little more explicit about who some of these other writers are: "He is loath," says Jonson, "to make nature afraid in his plays, like those that beget *Tales, Tempests* and such-like drolleries." Shakespeare knew all about Jonson's theory, and one wonders whether there is something deliberate in Shakespeare's avoidance of Jonson's formulas, almost as though he had a counter-theory of his own.

From *Transactions of the Royal Society of Canada*, XLVI (1952), pp. 47–58. Copyright by the Royal Society of Canada. Reprinted by permission of the author and the publisher.

At any rate, Jonson and Shakespeare have often been thought of as forming a kind of antithesis, and some of the fallacies from this over-simplified view of them are still with us. The contrast between a ponderous learned Jonson and a quick but ignorant Shakespeare is a myth based on an abortive seventeenth-century joke cycle, which comes to us through Fuller. There is better evidence that Jonson was a laborious writer and Shakespeare a fluent one, and it is clear that Jonson was more interested in the theory of criticism. On this basis many of us tend to think of Jonson and Shakespeare as respectively the sophisticated student of art and the inspired child of nature. True, as we have seen, Jonson was certain that he followed nature better than Shakespeare did. But since the rise of primitivism, the conception of "nature" has become less Aristotelian and more outdoorsy, and so Shakespeare's comedies, which lend themselves admirably to open-air performance, seem more natural than ever. With the triumph of the novel over the drama as a form of fiction, the criticism of drama became full of assumptions derived from the novel. Hence the frequent assertion that Jonson's characters are "flat" and Shakespeare's "round" — especially, of course, Falstaff.

This is, of course, nonsense; but neither do I agree that the difference between the two kinds of comedy is simply a difference between two kinds of artists — in other words that the difference is not a problem. The reason why I think there is a problem is that Jonson seems to have been so utterly right, as far as the history of the stage is concerned. All the important writers of English comedy since Jonson (except Barrie) have cultivated the comedy of manners with its realistic illusion and not Shakespeare's romantic kind. Nearly all of them have been Irishmen, and one might expect them to have a fey and Celtic sympathy for fairy-land; but from Congreve to O'Casey English comedy exhibits a remarkable dearth of leprechauns. Bernard Shaw remarked that the best way for a dramatist to get a reputation for daring originality is to stick as closely as possible to the method of Molière, whose comedy is more conventionalized even than Jonson's. As for the unities of time and place, many of us are graduated from college with a vague notion that they are useless and obsolete pedantries, and that Samuel Johnson or somebody proved it. Nevertheless the great majority of contemporary plays probably still observe them.

The tradition of Shakespearean comedy is very different. Since the closing of the theatres in 1642, it has survived chiefly in opera. As long as we have Mozart or Verdi or Sullivan to listen to, we can tolerate identical twins and lost heirs and love potions and folk tales: we can even stand a fairy queen if she is under two hundred pounds. But the main tradition of Shakespearean fantasy seems to have drifted from the stage into lyric poetry, an oddly bookish fate for the warbler of native woodnotes. Whitman was perhaps not wholly right when he wrote that Shakespeare's comedies "are altogether non-acceptable to America and democracy." Shaw was perhaps not wholly right when he suggested that many comedies of Shakespeare were pot-boilers, aptly described by such titles as *As You Like It* and *Much Ado About Nothing,* which could not hold the stage if Shakespeare were not a cultural vested interest. It was perhaps a wrong tendency to try to annex *All's Well* and *Measure for Measure* to the Jonsonian tradition by calling them "problem comedies," thus suggesting that for once in his life Shakespeare managed to produce something almost on a level with the weakest period of Ibsen. But still, when we look for the most striking parallels to *Twelfth Night* or *The Tempest,* we think, not of any dramatist, but of *Figaro* and *The Magic Flute.*

Jonson's comedy is one of the Renaissance developments of the Classical New Comedy that comes down from Plautus and Terence. The very slight modifications of this pattern in *cinquecento* Italian comedy need not be considered here. This form, though it is perhaps more of a formula, has been the ground plan of nearly all popular comedy down to our own time. Its most frequent theme is the approximation of a young man to a desirable young woman. The obstacles to this constitute the action of the comedy, and the overcoming of them the comic resolution. The obstacles are usually parental, and comedy often turns on a clash between a son's and a father's will. Thus the comic dramatist as a rule writes for the younger men in his audience, and the older members of almost any society are apt to feel that comedy has something subversive about it. This is certainly one element in the frequent social persecution of drama: in all the diatribes against the Elizabethan stage, no charge is more frequent than the corrupting of youth. Antagonism to comic drama is not peculiar to Puritans or even Christians: Terence in pagan Rome met much the same kind of social opposition that Jonson did. There is one scene in Plautus where a son asks his father pointedly if he really does love mother. Mr. Gilbert Norwood's book on Plautus speaks of this scene as a kind of ecstasy of bad taste, but one has to see it against the background of Roman family life to understand its importance as psychological release. Even in Shakespeare there are startling outbreaks of parallel ferocity. When Mr. Alfred Harbage speaks in his *As They Liked It* of the normal courtesy of Shakespeare's characters, the exceptions he finds to his rule are all concerned with the mockery of older men. In the movies, which provide the popular comedies of our own day, the triumph of youth is so relentless that the moviemakers are finding some difficulty in getting anyone over the age of seventeen into their audiences.

The opponent to the hero's wishes, when not the father, is generally someone who partakes of the father's closer relation to established society: that is, he is a rival with less youth and more money. In Plautus and Terence he is usually either the pimp who owns the girl, or a wandering soldier with a supply of ready cash. The fury with which these characters are baited and exploded from the stage shows that they are father-surrogates, and even if they were not, they would still be usurpers, and their claims to possess the girl must be shown up as somehow fraudulent. They are, in short, impostors, and the extent to which they have real power implies a criticism of the society that allows them their power. In Plautus and Terence this criticism seldom goes further than the fact that brothels are immoral; but in Renaissance dramatists, including Jonson, there is some sharp observation of the rising power of money and the sort of ruling class it is building up.

The action of comedy, therefore, consists normally in a clash of wills having for its aim the control of the comic society represented in the cast of characters. At first the characters who are thwarting the hero's triumph are in possession of social authority, and the audience realizes that this society is a Saturnalia or temporary inversion of the rightful society of the hero's triumph and their desires. When the obstacles are surmounted and the blocking characters reconciled or forced to submit, a new society is born on the stage. Its appearance is usually symbolized by some kind of party: a wedding, a banquet, as in *The Taming of the Shrew*, or a dance. Yet this new birth is also a rebirth, the return of the old normal society that the audience is accustomed to, and which has been for a moment usurped.

The defeated society, the group of ridiculous figures who dominate the action for the greater part of the play, are not essentially immoral, scoundrelly, or even hypocritical. They may be, but when they are the play represents a triumph of virtue over vice, and such a triumph belongs, not properly to comedy, but to melodrama, which attains its happy ending with a self-righteous moral tone that comedy avoids. In comedy the defeated characters are primarily ridiculous, and we have to inquire what, in this connection, the essence of the ridiculous is. It seems to be, from the general experience of comedy, the being confined to a certain type of behaviour, conditioned to act a single part. This brings us abreast of Jonson's conception of character in comedy as consisting of "humours."

A humour, Jonson tells us, is a character so possessed by a certain type of behaviour that he can act in no other way. A sick man is not a humour, but a hypochondriac is, because, *qua* hypochondriac, he can never admit to good health, and can never do anything inconsistent with being an invalid. All humours are possessed by what Pope calls a "ruling passion," and they are the opposite of the normal or temperate people who have their humours under control, like the hero and the audience. Jonson's theory applies to a great variety of characters; Molière's comedy is also a comedy of humours, but of a simpler type: he usually concentrates his actions on a single figure, a miser, a religious hypocrite, or a misanthrope, whose humour, or obsession, throws the whole society he controls into a perverted form. Jonson came nearest to this type of construction in *The Silent Woman*, where the whole action recedes from the humour of Morose, whose determination to eliminate noise from his life produces so uproariously garrulous a comic action. As we have said, humorousness, in Jonson's sense, represents not a moral but a social failure, and it often accompanies many virtues, as it does with Malvolio. But the judgment of comedy implies the supremacy of social over moral standards. Thus Molière's misanthrope is obsessed by the virtue of sincerity, only to discover (at least the audience discovers) that his friend Philinte, who is ready to lie quite cheerfully to enable other people to preserve their self-respect, is the more genuinely sincere of the two.

The humour is uniform rather than consistent, and the appeal of humours is based on one of the essential principles of comic writing: that unincremental repetition is funny. In a tragedy everything turns on a final catastrophe, and all repetition in tragedy — *Oedipus Rex* is the famous example — must lead emotionally and logically to that catastrophe. Laughter, however, is partly a reflex, and, like other reflexes, can be conditioned by a simple repeated pattern. In Synge's *Riders to the Sea* a mother's last son is drowned, and the result is a very beautiful and moving play. But if it had been a five-act tragedy plodding glumly through the whole seven drownings one after another, the audience would have been helpless with laughter long before the end. The same principle may be observed in comic strips and radio programmes, which, as they deal with static characters and an interminable form, can do nothing but repeat. A humour is established as a miser or a glutton or a shrew, and after the point has been made every day for several months it begins to be amusing. The girth of Falstaff and the obsession of Don Quixote may be at the other end of art, but they are based on the same comic laws. Mr. E. M. Forster speaks with great disdain of Dickens' Mrs. Micawber, who never says anything except that she will never desert her husband. We see here the contrast in taste between a minor comic writer too finicky for popular formulas, and a major one who exploits them ruthlessly.

There are certain stock types of comic humours, which persist with the most amazing tenacity all through the history of the stage. The earliest extant comedy, *The Acharnians* of Aristophanes, presents the swaggering soldier or *miles gloriosus,* who is still going strong in Shaw's *Arms and the Man* and Chaplin's *Great Dictator*. The hero of the same early play, who constructs the whole dramatic action himself, belongs to a type made famous by Prospero, but which turned up only the other day in the psychiatrist of Eliot's *Cocktail Party*. The parasite who appears in O'Casey's *Juno and the Paycock* is another type practically unchanged in twenty-five centuries.

As for the victorious society, the main figures are of course the technical hero and heroine, the nice young man and the nice young girl he finally gets. We find, from Plautus to the movies, that these central characters of comedy are seldom very interesting people. The young men (*adulescentes*) in Plautus and Terence are all alike, and even Shakespeare's heroes reflect a real technical difficulty, surmounted sometimes in a way that looks like a dodge. Thus the nice young men of *Much Ado* and *All's Well*, Claudio and Bertram, are dramatically interesting only because they are not very nice young men. In *The Merry Wives* the technical hero, a man named Fenton, has only a bit part, and this play has picked up a hint or two from Plautus's *Casina*, where the hero and heroine are not even brought on the stage at all. Ben Jonson, of course, follows the same pattern. There is a nice young man in *Volpone* named Bonario, but he is a nuisance, and his type is eliminated from the later great comedies, to their advantage. It is the same in Molière: everyone knows who Tartuffe and Harpagon are, but it is very hard to distinguish all the Valentins and Angéliques who wriggle out of their clutches. The hero's character has the neutrality which enables him to represent a wish-fulfilment. That is, we have to believe him to be a more interesting and important person than he is represented.

Whatever tragedy is, it has something to do with a vision of law, of what is and must be. It is parallel to the scientific vision, and it cannot be an accident that the two great developments of tragedy, in fifth-century Athens and seventeenth-century Europe, coincided with the two great revolutions in science. But when in a tragedy of Euripides the gods descend into the action and set things right, something fundamentally irrational has been brought into the vision of law, something which may lead even to the happy ending of comedy, as in *Alcestis*. Tragic endings impress us as true, and the suspense of tragedy is simply the waiting for an inevitable moment, like a predicted eclipse. But there is no such thing as inevitable comedy. Happy endings do not impress us as true, but as desirable, and they are brought about by deliberate manipulation. The watcher of death has nothing to do but sit and watch: the watcher of birth is a member of a busy society.

The comic ending is generally manipulated by a twist in the plot. In Roman comedy the heroine, who is usually a slave or courtesan, turns out to be the daughter of somebody respectable, so that the hero can marry her without loss of face. This type of ending is called a *cognitio* or recognition, in Greek *anagnorisis,* and is present whenever the final scene of a comedy turns on a lost heir found, the return of a rich forgotten relative, or a nurse with a retentive memory for birthmarks. There is a brilliant parody of a *cognitio* at the end of *Major Barbara,* where Undershaft is enabled to break the rule that he cannot appoint his son-in-law as successor by the fact that the son-in-law's own father married his deceased wife's sister in Australia, so that the son-in-law is his own first cousin as well as himself. It sounds complicated, but the plots of comedy often are complicated because there is something inherently absurd about complications. This is one reason for the convention of disguise. It should be noticed too that, as the main character interest in comedy is focussed on the defeated characters, comedy regularly illustrates a victory of arbitrary plot over consistency of character.

The manipulation of the plot does not always involve metamorphosis of character, but there is no violation of comic decorum when it does. Irrational conversions, miraculous transformations, and providential assistance are inseparable from comedy. The conversion of Oliver in *As You Like It,* or of the Agents of Don John in *Much Ado,* to say nothing of Katharina the shrew, strain our credulity even more than our heart-strings. Further, whatever emerges is supposed to be there for good. If the boy gets the girl, they are going to live happily ever after: if the curmudgeon becomes lovable, we are given to understand that he will not relapse. It is perhaps not surprising that Bernard Shaw, who must now be called the greatest comic dramatist of the age just before ours, should be interested in such subjects as creative evolution, social revolution, the advent of the Superman, and whatever metabiology is. Civilizations which stress the desirable rather than the real, and the religious as opposed to the scientific perspective, think of drama almost entirely in terms of comedy. In the classical drama of India the tragic ending was regarded as bad taste, much as the manipulated endings of comedy are regarded as bad taste by novelists interested in scientific realism.

One reason why there is such an emphasis on conversion is that the natural tendency of comedy is to include as many characters as possible in the new society of its final scene. Comedy delivers us from humours, not from villains, and if we treat a humour too much like a villain, he becomes pathetic, and the audience's sympathy switches over to him. Even Shylock, whose humour of carving up his debtors with a knife goes a little beyond the merely ridiculous, is pathetic, and nearly upsets the balance of tone. If his dramatic importance is ever so slightly exaggerated, as it generally is when the leading actor of the company takes the role, he does upset it, and the play becomes simply the tragedy of the Jew of Venice. The same thing is far more true of the character whose chief function has been to amuse the audience, especially the braggart. The original *miles gloriosus* in Plautus is a son of Jove and Venus who has killed an elephant with his fist and seven thousand men in one day's fighting. In other words, he is trying to put on a good show: the exuberance of his boasting helps to put the play over. The convention says that the braggart must be exposed, ridiculed, swindled, and beaten. But why should a professional dramatist, of all people, want so to harry a character who is putting on a good show — *his* show at that? Comedy, unlike tragedy, seems to move logically up toward the final curtain call in which all the characters are equally applauded. The word "plaudite" at the end of a Roman comedy would seem out of place in a tragedy, even if the applause itself would not. Hence, when we find Falstaff invited to the final feast in *The Merry Wives,* Caliban reprieved, and Angelo and Parolles allowed to forget their disgrace, we are seeing a fundamental principle of comedy at work.

If we look at tragedy, we can see that it has, so to speak, a positive and a negative pole. At one end is a feeling of acceptance and of the rightness of the tragedy; at the other is a feeling of the incongruity and wrongness of it. Combined, they make up the paradox of pity and terror which is tragedy. Desdemona arouses pity and Iago terror, but the central tragic figure is Othello, and our feelings about him are mixed. The negative pole of tragedy, the sense of wrongness, we call irony, and the positive pole is best described as heroism, the fact that the hero is big enough to make tragedy appropriate to him. All tragedies contain irony; unheroic or social tragedy, as we get it in Chekhov or Thomas Hardy, is primarily ironic. Irony thus contributes to tragedy the theme of the frustration of heroic action. The proportion of heroism to irony in a tragedy may obviously vary a good deal, the general rule being that sophistication increases the irony. Euripides has clearly a higher proportion of irony than Aeschylus or Sophocles, and he expresses this interest by displacing the centre of dramatic action from the tragic hero. Thus *Medea* is the tragedy of Jason, but the drama gains in ironic content by being focussed on the figure of Medea, the escaping avenger. In *Hippolytus* the moral paradox in the tragic situation — the hybris of excessive virtue — achieves a similar displacement.

It is clear that one step further would bring us to ironic comedy, the vision of human action as bound to a set pattern of repeating itself without getting anywhere. In other words, tragedy and comedy have, in irony, the same negative pole. In Shakespeare's canon there is one completely ironic play, *Troilus and Cressida,* and taking it as our ironic norm, we can see how the tragedies recede from it on one side and the comedies on the other. *Hamlet* and *Timon of Athens,* especially the latter, are nearest it among the tragedies. *Hamlet,* like *Hippolytus,* has a moral paradox at its heart, being an ironic treatment of a Senecan revenge play, and in *Timon* the ironic feeling that the hero's death has somehow failed to make a genuinely heroic point is very strong. Timon is oddly isolated from the final scene, dropping out of the action like Icarus in Breughel's picture, while the community he rejected closes up over his head. The contrast with the more typical tragedies, where nobody is allowed to steal the show from the tragic hero, needs no labouring. *Measure for Measure* and *All's Well* occupy a similar place on the ironic side of comedy: the former is a play in which all the male characters are threatened with death and yet nobody gets hurt, which makes it a tragi-comedy in the Elizabethan sense. Now as tragedy recedes from irony it becomes more heroic, until we get pure hero-plays like *Henry V* which are no longer real tragedies. What is the corresponding positive pole of comedy? Comedy, said Renaissance critics, is *imitatio vitae, speculum consuetudinis, et imago veritatis.* Irony in comedy is clearly *speculum consuetudinis,* the way of the world, *cosi fan tutte.* In what sense can comedy be *imago veritatis* as well, and what is its positive image of reality?

Let us return to our point that comedy is normally an erotic intrigue blocked by some opposition and resolved by a twist in the plot known as "discovery" or recognition. There are two ways of developing this pattern: one is to throw the weight of dramatic interest on the blocking figures, and the other is to throw it on the final discovery. The former direction is that of Jonson, Molière and their tradition; the latter is that of the romantic comedy of Shakespeare, with its folklore plots and fairy worlds, its coincidences and disguises, and its long final scenes of reconciliation, forgiveness, and wholesale marriage. As the Jonsonian tradition is ironic in its emphasis, it is obviously in Shakespeare that we should look for the *imago veritatis.*

In Shakespeare, unlike Jonson, the comic contest is usually presented as a collision of two societies. What corresponds to Jonson's social order of the humours is in Shakespeare a world depicted as similar to our own, but subject to an obviously absurd law, the law of killing strangers in the *Comedy of Errors,* of compulsory marriage in *A Midsummer Night's Dream,* the law that confirms Shylock's bond, or the attempts of Angelo to legislate people into righteousness. Sometimes the absurd law takes the simpler form of a tyrant like the humorous Duke Frederick or the mad Leontes. This once established, the action normally moves into a strange and yet oddly familiar wonderland, the wood of Puck and Oberon, the forest of Arden, Portia's house in Belmont, the pastoral retreat of Perdita, and from there the comic resolution is brought to birth. The bondage of humorous law is defeated by another kind of community, a world sufficiently strong to enter the so-called real world and impose its form on it. Outside the theatre, this second society is the simply unreal world of the dream in which desire is irresistible. It is only in comedy like Shakespeare's that we understand how it determines the form of our waking actions. The positive pole of comedy, then, seems to be a dream of an ideal society, not a formulated ideal, but a vision of what you will, the world as you like it. Just as comic irony is the social counterpart of tragic irony, so the "revel" of comedy is the social counterpart of heroism.

The world of the absurd law is headed for tragedy, and in almost any comedy we may become aware of having been delivered from tragedy. Even in laughter itself the element of release from the horrible seems to be important. The tricky slave who carries out the comic resolution in Roman comedy is regularly threatened with the most appalling tortures if he should fail: we might refer this simply to the brutality of Roman life until we remember that boiling oil and burying alive turn up in *The Mikado. The Cocktail Party* and *The Lady's Not for Burning* are civilized and high-spirited comedies of the contemporary theatre, but the cross appears in the background of the one and the stake in the background of the other. Shylock's knife and Angelo's gallows appear in Shakespeare, but as Shakespeare goes on he tends to put the tragic symbol nearer to the beginning of the comedy. The late romances are comedies that *contain* tragedies instead of simply avoiding them. *The Tempest* is a comedy of intrigue turned inside out, as it were, in which all the materials both of comedy and of tragedy are brought together and allowed to find their own levels.

People go to a theatre to be delighted and instructed, in that order, but the proportion may vary in different forms. In tragedy the instruction, the sense of being awakened to reality rather than pleasantly entertained, is at its strongest. It comes as something of a shock to realize that the blinding of Gloucester in *Lear* is still entertainment, the more so as the pleasure we get from it obviously has nothing to do with sadism. It was the great philosophical significance of tragedy, as a means of apprehending reality, that attracted Aristotle's attention to it, and the influence of Aristotle has been reinforced by a critical snobbery that puts tragedy, along with epic, at the top of an imaginary aristocracy of forms because it deals with ruling-class figures. The prestige of tragedy helped the parallel tradition of Aristotelian realism in Jonsonian comedy. In this comedy one notes a recurrent tendency to harangue and even scold audiences, warn them against relapses of taste, and insist that if dramatists must please to live, audiences have some cultural obligations too. The arrogance of Jonson and Congreve, the ridicule of bourgeois sentiment in Goldsmith and Shaw, the crusade against patriotic stereotypes in Synge and O'Casey, belong to a consistent pattern.

Molière had to please his king, but was not temperamentally an exception.

Shakespeare's comedy, which reaches its final form in the dramatic romance, is far more primitive and popular, and is of a type found all over the world. The conventions of romantic comedy are much the same whether we find them in *Cymbeline* or *The Winter's Tale*, in Fletcher or Lope de Vega, in the *commedia dell' arte* or the uninhibited plots of Italian opera, in Menander, in Kalidasa, in Chinese comedies of the Sung dynasty, in Japanese *kabuki* plays. If archaeologists ever discover a flourishing drama in Mayan or Minoan culture, it may not have plays like *Lear* or *Oedipus*, but it will assuredly have plays like *Pericles*. The contemporary commercial movie is much closer to Shakespearean romance than to the comedy of manners, and the various disrespectful Hollywood synonyms for discovery, "gimmick," "weenie" and the like, show clearly where its main interest lies. It looks as though the romance is actually the primitive and popular basis of dramatic entertainment, all other forms being specialized varieties of it. Even the operatic affinities of Shakespeare are not inconsistent with this suggestion: a Gilbert and Sullivan opera, considered as a comic structure, is more primitive and popular than a play of Shaw.

"Primitive" does not here mean chronologically early: the Old Comedy of Aristophanes, for all its horseplay and personal abuse and echoes of ritual, is a far more sophisticated kind of drama than the comedy of Menander. On the other hand, "popular" does not here mean giving an audience of the lower social ranks what it wants. Romantic comedy may be courtly, as in India, or bourgeois, as today, or classless, as it comes very near to being in Shakespeare. An audience's wants move horizontally in time: what it wants is a new variant of what pleased it before. The dramatist's wants move vertically in depth: he wants to achieve a profounder and clearer statement of what he said before. If Shakespeare at the end of his career reached the primitive and popular bedrock of drama, he did so as a result of giving the drama what it wanted, of expressing the laws of dramatic construction with increasing force and intensity. Jonson established, by conscious effort and will, the tradition of modern comedy; Shakespeare achieved a far deeper affinity with dramatic tradition in the manner recommended by some Chinese philosophers, by not doing anything about it.

11 (